Through the Soul Mirror to the Sphere of the Sun

André Consciência

Published by Falcon Books Publishing Ltd
Cover design by Tanya Robinson
Edited by Kendall Moore
First Printing: 2022

FALCON BOOKS PUBLISHING LTD
www.falconbookspublishing.com
Copyright © André Consciência 2022
All rights reserved.

ISBN: 978-1-8384598-7-1

Ordering Information:
Digital copies are available on the Falcon Books Publishing website:
www.falconbookspublishing.com

Dedication

XIX
The Trump of The Sun

'The Sun XIX,' from the Rider- Waite Tarot Deck

This book is dedicated to the tarot card 'The Sun', which depicts an infant riding a white horse under the anthropomorphised sun, with sunflowers in the background. The infant represents intellectual purity, the anthropomorphised sun represents godhood, the sunflower represents the adoration and loyalty of the heart towards godhood and the highest ideal, for the sunflower looks ever at the Sun. The white horse represents the spiritualisation of the magician's three bodies, mind, soul and physical, here depicted as the Unicorn, the Pegasus and the Horse. The card portends the good fortune, happiness, joy and harmony of the universe agreeing with the magician's path and aiding forward movement into something greater.

Preface

Igigi, the eleventh Earthzone spirit from Aries that is mentioned in *The Practice of Magical Evocation* by Franz Bardon, teaches us that to tame the Unicorn one must prepare him a crystal heart worked upon by remembering all instances of love by their purest essence to the extent that all obstacles to love are no more and, deeper still, they never were and never will be. The Unicorn is also called by the name of Pure Will.

To tame the Pegasus, said Igigi,

One must not direct it, instead, one's job is to not fall from the beast's lap. The Pegasus is a free heart. To tame it, the courage to follow it is enough. Yet, unless truth makes the rider light as a feather, he will keep falling, and the higher he goes, the greater he will descend.

Finally, Igigi says that to tame the Horse, one has to hold a firm grip of authority and knowledge together with the sensibility to provide. The Horse is as free as the Pegasus and as focused as the Unicorn, but he has mortal limitations and the master of the Horse must be trustworthy in his dealings with the universal laws.

Table of Contents

Introduction

This book follows up on the trail of Franz Bardon's *Initiation Into Hermetics,* applying his techniques used in the soul mirror training in Step 1 and I have further elaborated upon them.

The soul mirror is what distinguishes Bardon's system of hermetic training from all other training systems of hermeticism or magic, for, having dominion over his own mind and soul, the magician is already a master in any exercise he might attempt. Introspection is an essential ingredient to the formula, for, without it, he hasn't yet identified his mind or soul, to begin with. An Olympic champion cannot perform without perfect knowledge of his anatomy, for devoid of such knowledge, his anatomy will trick him into failing or else it will break in its own structure and destroy the athlete.

The practitioner is, thus, expected to have built his soul mirror, white and black, before proceeding with the work in hand. But, to start with, we will ask him to rearrange it into a second soul mirror category according to the most basic instincts whose credits humanity ignores when attributing the real causes of his actions. We think this is a key to the roots of not only many problems, but also solutions concerning the different virtues and faults, and connects the magician directly to the evolution of mankind as a whole so that, while he is working on his individuality, he is also working for the evolution of mankind. This structure is inspired by Nema's table of correspondences for what she calls, 'The Forgotten Ones[1]' and suffers from the author's own adaptations.

It is expected, then, that the magician already holds Bardon's *Initiation Into Hermetics* ("IIH") in his hands, as this is something we want to make sure of. *Through the Soul Mirror to the Sphere of the Sun* is suitable even for those who have not done any exercises in IIH. However, it is important that the magician, male or female, is able to read from our

---

[1] Nema (Margaret C. Ingall) was the founder of the Horus-Maat Lodge in 12/03/78. These are notes taken from her contemplations.

source directly. This book is also appropriate for the mature adept. It doesn't matter if he has completed IIH, *The Practice of Magical Evocation, The Key to True Quabbalah* or any system of magic foreign to Franz Bardon, as any may benefit greatly from it and take heed of the sphinx's words,

Man, if you wish to know the Gods and the Universe, know thyself.

otes on the Primal Instincts

Notes on the Primal Instincts Called
"The Forgotten Ones[2]"

Let us start with something more likely familiar to the dear hermetic reader, *The Corpus Hermeticum*[3] by Hermes Trismegistus, where we are introduced to the twelve irrational tormentors of the body. They spring from the lack of reason in the collective. They are:

1. Ignorance
2. Grief
3. Intemperance
1. Concupiscence
2. Injustice
3. Avarice
4. Deceit
5. Envy
6. Treachery
7. Anger
8. Recklessness
9. Malice

These are considered to be root tormentors, meaning that from them derive other tormentors, although Hermes states that there are many others. What they have in common is that they make use of the senses in order to create suffering and imprisonment, and they are what Bardon calls vices, faults and weaknesses. That is, his concept of the Black Mirror which is the mirror of such tormentors. The decipher will understand, by hints given by Hermes, that each of these tormentors corresponds to a sign

---

2 Notes by Nema, "The Forgotten Ones".

3 Hermes Trismegistus, *The Corpus Hermeticum, XIII. The Secret Sermon on the Mountain* http://gnosis.org/library/hermes13.html.

in the zodiac. Against such tormentors, the hermeticist has ten powers of God that cleanse the body and soul. This corresponds to the White Mirror in *Initiation Into Hermetics*[4].

The 10 powers are:

1. Gnosis
2. Joy
3. Self -Control
4. Perseverance
5. Justice
6. Unselfishness
7. Truth
8. Goodness
9. Life
10. Light

What happens is that:

- Gnosis dissipates ignorance
- Joy dissipates grief
- Self-control dissipates intemperance
- Perseverance and patience dissipates concupiscence
- Justice dissipates injustice
- Unselfishness dissipates avarice
- Truth dissipates deceit
- Life dissipates anger and recklessness
- Light dissipates envy and treachery
- Goodness dissipates malice

In addition, let us explain a little further about root traits and their passive and negative matrices. Hermes states that Truth, Life and Light are the triune, since they are one. *The Corpus Hermeticucm* seems to suggest that this triune by itself being God in structure, is capable of chasing away the tormentors of darkness. From these three virtues, spring forward the

---

[4] Bardon, F. *Initiation into Hermetics*.(Germany: Rüggeberg-Verlag, 1993).

11

other eight virtues, when all ten virtues[5] are complete in the soul of the hermeticist, he is born spiritually into the divine. Here, Light is the active power and Life is the passive power which is to say, that Life happens on its own and self-regulates, but the Light is self-created and self-generated.

Now, in the *Corpus Hermeticum,* we also see that some tormentors are together and depend on each other, such as envy and treachery, anger and recklessness. Treachery consecrates its practitioner as an initiate in the mysteries of envy and once anger has made the practitioner reckless, guilt will incorporate anger in his conscience. Recklessness and treachery are passive traits. They are meant to regulate envy and anger, which are active traits. The most common strategy to combat an active trait is by willpower and transmutation. But take one away and the other will soon become a frail and simple shade.

Let us go to Book I[6], for the way things are described there connects deeply with Nema's vision, but we will get to it in due time. One can find these words in the *Corpus Hermeticum:*

> *The form you had becomes unseen, and you surrender to the divine power your habitual character, now inactive. The bodily senses return to their own sources. Then they become parts again and rise for action, while the seat of emotions and desire go to mechanical nature.*

It goes on to explain how one climbs through the planetary spheres leaving behind different vices. These spheres are as layers of our inner being, like layers of an onion. In the foundations we leave impermanence, to get to splendour we sacrifice our machinations, to get to victory we sacrifice the illusion of longing, to get to beauty we sacrifice arrogance, to get to rigour we sacrifice presumption, to get to mercy we sacrifice hoarding and to understand we sacrifice falsehood. *The Corpus Hermeticum* doesn't mention such virtues, only the corresponding planets,

---

[5] One should consider that Life and Light function as one. Therefore they are both eleven and ten virtues.

[6] Hermes Trismegistus Book 1 Vol1 *Poimandres to Hermes, The Shepherds of Men,* https://www.coum.org/wp-content/uploads/2017/10/Poimandres-to-HermesV2.pdf

but here I have given another example of a White Mirror and of a Black Mirror, and of how they can interact.

At Maat Magick, Nema states:

> *Initiation continues, but the individual identity and collective identity do not. There are three more levels of rarity to attain, but they lie beyond the realm of duality, beyond your faith in your new reality...In a type of reverse gestation, your levels 9 through 4[7] deconstruct themselves into spiritual dust. Your 10th level[8] continues its business in the world, functioning on its memory of perfection.*

The aim of Nema's master book, *Maat Magick*, is similar to the aim of the *Corpus Hermeticum*. In the mystical component of her path to adepthood she uses virtues of the levels or planetary spheres in her attempt to control and reabsorb the unbalanced survival urges that have taken autonomy in the ego-consciousness. She calls these urges by the name of "The Forgotten Ones". At the dawning of life on our planet there was hunger, from hunger the urge to survive developed the mask of sex, then of fight-or-flight, clanning, speech, curiosity, altruism and, finally, of God-hunger.

The last one, God-hunger, can be defined as the human impulse towards transcendence. Hunger is basic to the individual. Sex is basic to the species. Fight or flight is the basic instinct of fear and risk-taking. To make a living and to stay alive we find it necessary to band with others, and that's clanning, of which they say, "Blood is thicker than water". Up until now, we have been talking of reactive instincts, although clanning stands in-between reaction and action. Active instincts are altruism, communication and curiosity. Communication is the social glue of stored knowledge capable of expanding clanning and of surviving from generation to generation. Curiosity is the driver of our mystery of transformation, and it is curiosity which discovers the benefits of altruism. Altruism can either

---

[7] Moon through Jupiter.

[8] Physical reality.

make you a hero or a victim of all kinds, but it is this 'Forgotten One' that can expand the self.

To explain the Forgotten One of God-hunger, I shall expound upon this so that the reader can understand how these base instincts are irrational and unconscious forces capable of building consciousness.

- **Eating:** we begin to acknowledge that the outer world is also us.
- **Through Sexual desire:** we learn that there is a special affinity with the ones closest to us being us.
- **Fight or flight:** makes us fear the unknown, for the unknown isn't us, and it brings about the thirst for knowledge.
- **Clanning:** makes us relate with intelligence as an entity and a quantity, for us to abide socially we need a learning attitude. Communication allows us to realise that we are not only what we absorb but also that which we transmit, and has us praying to the unknown; curiosity makes us realise that the path to the unknown can be found by the truth.
- **Altruism:** has us identifying finally with the cosmic consciousness of the intelligence of truth - the highest good.
- **God-hunger:** arises as a fever from the realisation that we are an expression of what we now seek.

These are eight dualistic urges, but the eighth is a gateway between dualism and non-dualism. Nema is not using the twelve main tormentors, as the *Corpus Hermeticum* does, but seven survival instincts divided by the chakras and the planets as layers of existence. This is not that black and white. But what are they, exactly? In 1983 Sor .'. [9] Nema published the article called, "Foundation". This was, if I'm correct, the first time she mentions 'The Forgotten Ones'.

> *Another feature of the Astral planes is the access to the Forgotten Ones. These entities are, basically, the gods of our genetic structure. They are the successful survival-factors that have been covered, in the individual and racial Unconscious, with the veneer of conscious Mind and civilization.*

[9] The Cincinnati Journal of Ceremonial Magick, vol I number 5.

Later, she continues.

The Forgotten Ones are of Man's origins and assisted us from the ocean to the cave. However, for a certain span of our unrecorded history, our survival-force was controlled and employed by entities from "beyond" our Universe... Alien beyond human imagining, they cannot truthfully be construed as evil. Their main purpose is to devour, and since their structure is incomparable with "our" Universe's physics, they can but eat by means of the life-forms native to our Universe.

In this form of magical mythology, she teaches us that the so-called 'Forgotten Ones' are both our allies and our enemies, just like the black mirror is our true guide. These primal instincts or 'Forgotten Ones' give us skills, virtues and powers by way of sublimation, but they are ready to destroy a malformed complexification back to dust.

In her article, Nema proceeds to give some suggestions on how to deal with the Forgotten Ones, suggestions that may as well be valuable to our readers.

The Magickian should be extremely cautious to maintain his consciousness at the balance between the suspension of Rational Mind and the detached surveillance of his actions by his Observer.

While the Forgotten Ones are in this way invited to express themselves freely, leaving less and less of the magician's sense of self, she then applies her technique of the black flame, similar to the vacancy of mind and the akashic trance of Bardon combined, nothing remaining. Then, she explains:

In subsequent daily experience, he will become aware that a new balance has been struck. He has a new sense of unity with the undercurrents of the life-flow and will find this of great use in nonverbal communication with others. Through his Art he will establish links with the Unconscious of others; he will assist them to meet the Forgotten Ones in controlled circumstances that will do no harm. He is also ready to begin work on a world-scale. The Forgotten Ones have access to Man on the astral planes, mainly in the dream-state. Those sections of humanity who exist in starvation conditions, in poverty that has practically negated civilised consciousness, are the hunger-gates of the Forgotten Ones. These starvelings have thin, if indeed any, barriers between the waking (reason) and dreaming (primal drive) states. Their physical strength may be too depleted for the bearing of arms, but theirs is the massed power of the Forgotten Ones. The demon-conflicts of the fortunate nations (the "chosen" of the bright gods) are petty when compared with the dark powers gathering within the hunger of the starving.

In the hope that such notions have further clarified our concept of the soul mirrors and the use of the 'Forgotten Ones', we shall move forward.

We have discussed two mirrors made in the image of mankind's instincts. On the alternative black mirror, we will, therefore, place some of these instincts, and on the white mirror, the powers and virtues that sublimate them or that arise out of their sublimation. When the magician has read Bardon's take on the soul mirror, he may follow with us at the start of this long journey, being sure that he will be able to understand the words and their intrinsic logic.

Black Mirror Root Instincts

Element	Active Root	Passive Root
Fire	Fight or Flight	God-hunger
Air	Speech	Curiosity
Water	Clanning	Altruism
Earth	Sex	Hunger

- The fire element represents fight-or-flight as an active root and God-hunger as a passive root.
- The air element represents speech as the active root and curiosity as the passive root.
- The water element represents clanning as the active root and altruism as the passive root.
- The earth element represents sex as the active root and hunger as the passive root.

White Mirror Root Powers and Virtues

Element	Active Root	Passive Root
Fire	Command and Speed	Transcendence
Air	Communication	Discernment
Water	Bonding and Love	Compassion
Earth	Allure & Fascination	Stability & Learning

- The fire element represents command and speed as the active roots and transcendence as the passive root.
- The air element represents communication as the active root and discernment as to the passive root.
- The water element represents bonding and love as the active roots and compassion as the passive root.
- The earth element represents allure and fascination as the active roots and stability and learning as the passive roots.

The instincts in the black mirror communicate among themselves, and the powers and virtues in the white mirror do the same. Additionally, white and black mirrors interact not only individually but globally to cause balance through cause and effect in the world at large. The faults include inadequate responses to the outlined instincts and the virtues adequate responses to the powers derived from those instincts. We will later change the scale and our root references, for we intend to make this work as a system of practical magick and initiation into adepthood. But for now, we will leave the reader with an example, so that while he is purifying and balancing the elements on himself he is also working with the root and global instincts.

The attributes with which we fill our tables are but a starting point: remember that Franz Bardon speaks of at least 100 faults and 100 qualities, and has the magician complete the writing of the soul mirror in the course of two weeks.

Black Mirror Trait Examples

Hunger (Earth Element)

Active Faults
Hunger Excess:
need
selfishness
excess
greed
avarice
gluttony
miserliness
hoarding

Passive Faults
Lack of Hunger:
apathy
sloth
neglecting health

Unspecified:
famine
death
hungry pangs

Sex (Earth Element)

Active Faults
Sexual Excess:
distraction
lack of honour
lack of words,
lack of control
lack of self-preservation
lack of enlightened self
interest
lust
obsession

Passive Faults
Sexual Lack:
tension
dissatisfaction
being overly cerebral
being overly acquisitive
excessive engagement in control of behaviour
giving too much attention to others
being manipulative

Unspecified
pestilence
death
sexually transmitted diseases
sexual heat

Fight or Flight (Fire Element)

Active Faults
thievery
hatred
vindictiveness

Passive Faults
jealousy
anger

Unspecified
adrenaline rush
panic
vertigo

Clanning (Water Element)

Active Faults
excess
clanning
compliance
shyness

Passive Faults
lack
indifference
frigidity
negligence
laziness

Unspecified
social formatting

Speech (Air Element)

Active Faults
boasting

Passive Faults
frivolity

Curiosity (Air Element)

Active Faults
gossiping

Passive Faults
irascibility
melancholy

God Hunger (Fire Element)

Active Faults
insolence

Passive Faults
instability
lack of conscience
irregularity

Unspecified
anomaly
dullness

Altruism (Water Element)

Active Faults
self-presumption

Passive Faults
squandering
curiosity

White Mirror Trait Examples

Sublimated Hunger (Earth Element)

Active Powers
learning
respect

Passive Powers
stability
responsibility

Sublimated Sex (Earth Element)

Active Powers
allure
tenderness

Passive Powers
fascination
fervency

Sublimated Fight or Flight (Fire Element)

Active Powers
command
firmness

Passive Powers
Speed
activity
enthusiasm

Sublimated Clanning (Water Element)

Active Powers
love

Passive Powers
kindness

Sublimated Speech (Air Element)

Active Powers
communication
conscientiousness

Passive Powers
sobriety

Sublimated Curiosity (Air Element)

Active Powers
bonding
diligence
discernment
dexterity

Passive Powers
abstemiousness

Sublimated God-hunger (Fire Element)

Actives Powers
transcendence
lust

Passive Powers
tranquillity

Sublimated Altruism (Water Element)

Active Powers
compassion
forgiveness

Passive Powers
modesty

As long as the magician keeps in mind that this is a raw example, he should remain free to create his soul mirror tables as honestly as possible, for it is a matter of the individual. He is to keep in mind at all times that there may be different types of, for instance, lust. Some are qualities and some are deficiencies, and also the same type of lust may manifest in different elemental tables and through different instincts, or it may be, at the same time, a virtue and a fault, in which case the magician is to understand where the dividing line lies.

Step 1

Step one is dedicated to those exercises to be done before working directly with the soul mirror as Franz Bardon describes it. They should prepare the magician to readily face the challenges ahead and with less effort, stress and tension on his part.

Previously we have discussed the analogy from the Sun Tarot. We will use this to illustrate the 3 bodies, namely the mind, soul/astral and physical bodies. The white Horse represents the spiritualisation of the magician's three bodies. Mind, soul and physical here are depicted as the Unicorn, the Pegasus and the Horse.

Taming of the Unicorn (The Mind)

The magician is to sit, relax, and let his mind drift, observing his thoughts but not interfering with them. He opens his eyes and writes down everything after 5 minutes. For seven days he repeats the procedure. After seven days he examines the diary and tries to capture patterns and repeated thoughts, even when they come in different shapes. The practitioner names these patterns and divides them into three layers (categories) of frequency, from the most recurring, to the least recurring, which are written in the diary under each element.

He will then attribute a word or words to these repeated thoughts. Some thoughts are more or less abstract. For instance, if a ball of light formed repeatedly in the mind of the magician during the exercise the most obvious words would be "ball" and "light", but if he digs further to find subdivisions he may find "sight", "clarity", "luminosity", "world", "planet", "sphere" and even "manifestation" or "unity". The symbolic thoughts are the hardest, for they can divide into a variety of words. On the other hand, if the magician finds in his diary a pattern of irrational fears under different forms, the most important is not the shape in which it comes, but the root, that is, the fear and the irrational, and here he obtains two words. Surely, the word fear still contains "afraid", "fright", "scared", etc.

The magician starts with the less recurring patterns or thoughts and, in his speech, he is to avoid the words related to them. Every time he pronounces this word he is to pinch himself on the finger and draw a cross in this diary under the section of that word and its derivatives. Once a whole week has gone without him pronouncing a word and its variations, he erases it from his diary, and when the last word from the least recurring layer has been dominated, he jumps to the medium layer, and finally to the one with the most recurring thoughts.

Taming of the Pegasus (The Soul/Astral)

Now, in his daily life, the magician is to take notes every time he gets distracted from his present activities, and he is to nominate whatever has distracted him and the emotion connected to it. After seven days he gathers these emotions and divides them into three layers as before. He does not try to stop having these feelings, but he is to prevent them from distracting him. Again, he starts with the layer having the least recurring emotions and proceeds to pinch his hand and write down a cross under the column of the named emotion for every time it distracts him. When the layer with the most recurring distractions has no emotion left, he is ready to move on.

Taming of the Horse (The Physical Body)

To balance one's mental and emotional control and stop it from becoming oppressive one needs to have both a relaxed and an active and effective body. Our first suggestion concerning the physical plane is the practice of Chi Kung and cultivating this habit on a daily basis for at least 5 minutes a day, which will also refine his practice of conscious breath. We are not asking the magician to become a Chi Kung master, and it should be sufficient for him to acquire books on the matter, consult websites and watch videos that teach and show the practice of Chi Kung. It is also useful to say that the magician who is physically disabled is completely free to adapt my suggestions to his capacities to whatever extent needed.

Step 2

Taming of the Unicorn

Now it's time for the magician to start working directly with his soul mirror. The magician will divide his daily mental practice in two parts, one for the black mirror and one for the white mirror.

Black Mirror

He is to hold a chain of thoughts of a negative trait related to a root instinct or any of its subdivisions, depending on whether he wants to attack the root or start by attacking its parts. He holds this chain of thoughts and does not allow his thoughts to deviate from the matter for five to ten minutes a day, and at the end, he is to take notes on his reflections.

For example, if a recurring soul mirror trait is jealousy, the practitioner would meditate upon this for ten minutes noting the chain of thoughts related to that subject. He would then assign it to the relevant element root instinct be it passive or active. In this case, it would be assigned under the fire element as a passive trait (which is a subdivision of the root firefight or flight).

Using this method is two-fold, not only is the practitioner bringing awareness to the negative trait and allowing the mind to explore it more deeply, but also developing his skills of one-pointed focus on a subject required for step 2.

White Mirror

The same is to be done with the powers and virtues, the sublimated instincts. The magician will be able to close each trait when his reflections lead him to find the connection between a negative and a positive aspect.

This should be achieved with at least each of the passive and active roots of the black mirror. It may be that to his experience a root defect connects not to a root power or virtue, but to one of its subdivisions, or that he actually finds new positive traits under his scrutiny.

Taming of the Pegasus

Next, the magician is to fix his thoughts on the life source of each of the active and passive root powers and virtues of sublimated instincts. Nothing, except the subdivisions of a positive trait, may manifest on his mind, and they may only manifest as long as the firm presence of the root trait is never absent from the magician's firm concentration. Each session is to be dedicated to a single trait and should last from five to ten minutes without suffering distractions. As a sign of success, the magician will feel the sensation of becoming vacant and being filled by light with the quality of vibration in the power or virtue at hand. Once the magician has completed this quest in all aspects, using the bipolar method of thought control, he is to let his mind roam freely on the subject of an unbalanced root instinct while, at the same time, fixing his concentration and willpower on the sublimated instinct connecting to it, so that the latter starts to heal the thought pattern of the imbalance and to dissipate it at once.

Taming of the Horse

To the magician's exercises of Chi Kung, he is to add five minutes of Tai Chi Chuan. Again, it is not required for him to master the practice of Tai Chi to its limits, and he may remain at the beginner's stage. To our requirements, he has no necessity to acquire a personal master. The natural flow of things will have him advancing with tranquillity.

Step 3

Taming of the Unicorn

The magician concentrates on each of the negative traits, starting from the less present to the most present at each instinct, but this time his chain of thoughts is directed toward understanding how and why each trait differs from the magician himself. Once an active or a passive root has been ruled out by the magician's understanding that it is not him, and there is nothing left on his chain of thoughts, the magician fixes his mind in that same state where nothing remains for five to ten minutes. Then, when the whole black mirror is ruled out and the magician's being is rendered separate from it, he moves on to his virtues and powers and applies the same method.

Taming of the Pegasus

It is time to apply the mystery of breathing to the soul mirror. In Step 1 of IIH[10], Bardon writes:

> *If we put a thought, idea or an image, no matter whether it be concrete or abstract, in the air to be inhaled, it will take in the akasha principle of the air concerned, and convey it, through the electric and magnetic fluids, to the air substance. In the first place, the material parts of the elements are destined to preserve the body, secondly the elctro-magnetic fluid, charged with the idea or the image, will lead the electro-magnetic air cloured with the idea, from the blood-stream through the astral matrix, to the astral body, and from there to the immortal spirit through the reflective mental matrix.*

---

[10] Franz Bardon, *Initiation into Hermetics* (Germany: Rüggeberg-Verlag, 1993), 57-58.

And, later, he adds the magician should make himself comfortable, relax his entire body and breathe while imagining that the inhaled air brings health, calmness, contentment and success or whatever the magician is trying to achieve. The air, so imbued, passes through the lungs, blood and body consequently. Peace, success or whatever is to be achieved must be imagined intensely enough for the air inhaled to be impregnated with the wish as an ultimate and realised reality.

The image of the idea being inspired through the air is impregnated with the reality of the wish fulfilled in such a way that there is no doubt whatsoever about this fulfilment being a fact.

In this book, the magician is breathing in his virtue and breathing out the connected fault, and he will have as his ally the magical diary, where he has pointed out, before, how or where each virtue and vice connects. When the fault, deficiency, defect or vice dissipates entirely, he is to keep inhaling the virtue, quality or power, until he starts to feel its quality filling his blood. A sign of success is that the failures stop manifesting.

Additionally, the magician will add conscious reception of food and water magic. While conscious breathing is especially effective on more intellectual and mental traits, water magic is more effective on predominantly emotional traits, and the reception of food, strengthening of the body and healing of its unbalanced weakness, illness and addiction. Conscious drinking stands somewhere between water magic and the conscious reception of food so that green teas can be impregnated with earth virtues, white teas with water virtues, red and black teas with fire virtues, and simple water with virtues of the air. They can also be impregnated to purge corresponding faults and illnesses.

About the conscious reception of food, Bardon[11] writes that one should stand in front of his food and, with the greatest intensity of imagination, concentrate on his desire embodying the food as effectively as if indeed this desire has already been realised. The magician is then to eat slowly and consciously, having complete conviction that the desire is

---

[11] Franz Bardon, *Initiation into Hermetics* (Germany: Rüggeberg-Verlag, 1993), 59.

passing together with the food into the body down to the finest nerves. This is to be seen as a sacred act in line with the communion of Christianity.

On water magic,[12] Bardon says that every time we are washing our hands we should intensely think that by washing them we are equally washing the uncleanliness of our soul. Alternatively, we can magnetise and impregnate with our desire the water we are going to use. To this end, we remain completely convinced that by washing the power passes into the body, realising the desire.

The magician is now breathing, feeding and washing, hence making use of the three basic primal fundamentals for the accomplishment of his refined Great Work, that of Magical Equilibrium.

Taming of the Horse

To Chi Kung and Tai Chi, the magician now adds five extra minutes of training in the martial arts of Shaolin Kung Fu. This may be harder to practise, but it is sufficient for him to practise solo and the basics of Tai Chi might help him build little by little the basics of Shaolin, from stretching to the stances, hand drills, walking, hopping, jumping and kicking. Now, the magician has built a positive habit of exercising fifteen minutes a day.

---

[12] Franz Bardon, *Initiation into Hermetics* (Germany: Rüggeberg-Verlag, 1993), 61.

Step 4

Taming of the Unicorn

It is now time to learn conjuration. The Bardonist methods of autosuggestion and the secret of the subconscious come into play. Bardon tells us to remove time and space from the subconscious, imbue it with our desire and make a mala, using sentences that omit the use of words like "when" or "where", and therefore only using words that are in the present tense and manifesting presence. We have added into the sentences words of command that reinforce victory and the removal of time and space from the subconscious. While the magician is practising he may apply a "desire" that is efficient to any sentence: a feeling of electricity that feeds itself upon the sound of our voice, irradiating the light accumulation of absolute victory over time and space. The conjuration shall then direct this light to the different commands given. According to the draft we gave as an example, we will build a banishment against the faults of hunger.

- I omnipresently, eternally, supremely and totally, consciously and unconsciously, have an absolutely balanced appetite in all known and unknown ways.
- I eternally am, omnipresently, supremely and totally, consciously and unconsciously, absolutely self-sufficient in all known and unknown ways.
- I eternally am, omnipresently, supremely and totally, consciously and unconsciously, absolutely generous in all known and unknown ways.
- I eternally, omnipresently, supremely and totally, consciously and unconsciously, manifest bountifulness absolutely, in all known and unknown ways.
- I eternally, omnipresently, supremely and totally, consciously and unconsciously, manifest detachment absolutely, in all known and unknown ways.

- I eternally, omnipresently, supremely and totally, consciously and unconsciously, have absolute moderation, in all known and unknown ways.
- I eternally, omnipresently, supremely and totally, consciously and unconsciously, manifest absolute contentment in my life in all known and unknown ways.
- I omnipresently, eternally, supremely and totally, consciously and unconsciously, forever manifest paradise, in all known and unknown ways. In all known and unknown ways.
- I omnipresently, eternally, supremely and totally, consciously and unconsciously, find hoarding to be absolutely useless.
- I omnipresently, eternally, supremely and totally, consciously and unconsciously, manifest cheerfulness and there is an absolute initiative where I am.
- I eternally am omnipresently, supremely and totally, consciously and unconsciously healthy in all known and unknown ways.
- I am omnipresently immortal, eternally immortal, supremely and totally immortal, consciously and unconsciously immortal and maximum plenitude abides absolutely in my light in all known and unknown ways. So it is divinely and most superiorly decreed.

A conjuration like this is to be used at every instinct, incinerating its faults, and to every sublimated instinct, affirming and establishing its powers, qualities, skills and virtues. On the conjuration of the virtues, passive and active components of each section or division are to be mixed, for they fortify each other by building subtle electromagnetic volts. The conjuration is repeated and the magician moves the mala bead at each repetition, from sphere to sphere, until he is back at his starting point.

The hardest traits to dominate may suffer from a refinement of this technique that will render the subconscious even more defenceless against the efforts of the magician, for he may translate his conjuration into Enochian, preferably, or some of the so-called barbaric languages of magic. The subconscious will not be able to contradict the words and is rendered useless against the intention. A common solution is a translation to Latin, for as long as the magician is not a specialist of the dead language it will remain familiar enough to be intuitive to the magician but still irrational.

Latin does not need to be perfect, as knowing perfectly how to speak or write Latin isn't exactly the point in the present context.

Certain qualities may be encrypted in a manner that unites every Roman letter of their name into a single glyph, or they can be translated into Hebrew or Greek since Hebrew and Greek letters can function as sigils by themselves. Talismans can be made out of it and inserted into coins that the magician carries with him, grabs and moves between his fingers, reinforcing the presence of the virtue and sealing away the opposite fault. The translations can also be used with the magician's weaknesses if he inscribes the Hebrew or Greek letters in a circular fashion, like that of a clock and, carrying it on a paper card, keeps watch over his instincts, so that when the weakness starts to manifest he fights right away and stops it from acting. Each time he is able to do it, he erases one of the letters, until there are none left. But if he fails once, he has to do another paper card and start at the beginning. When he finishes, the talisman will be active against his faults.

Taming of the Pegasus

At this time the magician will personify his virtues and qualities into a character or a symbol. He should proceed with at least his main mother and father virtues and qualities at each sublimated instinct, that is, his main passive and active virtues, qualities, skills, etc. He is to look at the symbols carefully, close his eyes, and fix the images without them altering in any way for five to ten minutes. A sign of success is that the magician will feel the spiritual presence of that virtue filling him or manifesting in the space around him. Then he will repeat, but this time his eyes will be open. The image is not to vanish in any way for at least five minutes and, after that, a sign of success is that it starts expressing itself as if it is alive, due to the accumulation of astral light.

Then the magician will repeat his faults, this time drawing them necessarily as humans. He will practise with his eyes closed and never with his eyes opened. After he succeeds in stabilising the image, he is to ask his reason or intuition for an aspect that would change in the figure if it started to heal and to become virtuous. Such an aspect will probably manifest automatically in the image if the answer is intuitive, but if it is mostly rational, the magician is to make the changes consciously. Little by little, the figure of the vice will mutate into its healing form and the magician is to give it a new name. A sign of success is when the figure starts emanating a sense of divine grace and the memory of the vice is no more. The full image transfiguration of vices may be accomplished in a variety of sessions.

Now, he will pick another fault and associate it with a sound or a sound pattern. The other senses, such as sight, smell, taste and touch should not participate in this exercise. He is to listen to it as if it is real for at least five minutes, and if he has chosen a sound pattern he will add in other tones, harmonies and patterns until he finds an elevating symphony. If he has chosen a particular sound, such as the sound of an animal, of a cave or of burning fire, he is to add in other sounds that will put the sound he has first associated with his imbalance in a harmonious and transcendental context.

Now, let him pick a perfume that he associates with a certain virtue, and imagine its odour until it becomes real and established. If he picked an active virtue associated with a certain instinct or element, let him pick now a passive virtue and later combine both smells into a single perfume.

Let him go further with tastes, training one at a time and combining the four tastes particular to an element. He may make use of the active and passive roots of two sublimated instincts associated with one of the four elements.

Finally, let him practise sensory concentration, associating sensations to the elements themselves, such as cold to the water, heat to the fire, lightness to the air and pressure to the earth element. He will practise one at a time and later combine the four.

Let no sense lag behind, for the equilibrium of the four senses is as important as the equilibrium at the soul mirror.

Once these problems have been solved, the magician will again work with his imagination that would connect him to the power of his

39

virtues and strengths. He will imagine the visual personification of his virtues, strengths, and so on, and he will add in density, vibration, smell and taste to the image. When this is done and the virtue feels alive and radiating intelligence in the image, the magician starts to breathe it in through the pores. He breathes in the light that emanates from the figure, and the light is imbued with the smell, sensation, taste and sound vibration of the virtue or strength. When the magician breathes out, he is to imagine a shield forming around him against any opposite weakness or fault.

About pore breathing, Franz Bardon[13] writes that in each inspiration we should think that not only our lungs but the whole body, every single pore, is inhaling air, receiving vital power and conveying it to the body. When breathing in, the magician is to become a dry sponge when it urgently sucks the water. In this way, the magician has the vital power pass from the etheric principle to his surroundings and to himself. The fulfilment of desire is realised, therefore, through the whole body. Once some skill has been attained in this experiment, the magician learns to exhale magically by imagining at each breathing out that he is expelling the opposite of the desire.

Success will come when the magician's faults, weaknesses and defects that handicap his development have been erased from the black mirror and the soul mirror has become balanced.

Taming of the Horse

At this time the magician scales up and imagines the personification of the principles themselves within the four elements. That is:

- **The fire element:** sublimated God-hunger and sublimated fight-or-flight.
- **The air element:** sublimated speech and sublimated curiosity.
- **The water element:** sublimated clanning and sublimated altruism.
- **The earth element:** sublimated sex and sublimated hunger.

---

[13] Franz Bardon, *Initiation into Hermetics* (Germany: Rüggeberg-Verlag, 1993), 58.

He will ask them for a bodily position that represents them, and if he is working through intuition the figures themselves will answer and show him, but if he is using reason he is to research bodily postures and their symbolism and apply them to the plasmifications of these principles, fixing them on the asanas or bodily postures for five to ten minutes in his imagination, later taking notes about his impressions.

Next, he will assume such postures himself. If the principles are showing him postures impossible to master in the human body, he is to ask them to adjust the postures to his own body. He stays in the asanas from thirty minutes to one hour, and later takes notes, once again, on his impressions. Outstanding success is given when the magician spills no drop of sweat after thirty minutes or one hour in each of the positions. Nonetheless, let the magician be reminded that he should start slowly. There is no need for him to rush to thirty minutes at the earlier stages.

Step 5

The soul mirror, white and black, that the magician has mastered, is to be kept and monitored from time to time. But now, the magician is to work with a new soul mirror based on the four hermetic principles of knowing, willing, daring and keeping silent. And he is to apply everything that he has learned so far in mastering this mirror.

The mirror has its own rules and can be portrayed as follows:

Fire Principle: Volition
Root Virtue: Unshakable will
Subordinates: Toughness, patience and perseverance

The magician starts by mastering perseverance, then patience, and then toughness. Finally, he is rewarded with an unshakable will. The three subordinate virtues of the fiery unshakable will are of the earth element and maybe imagined with qualities of the earth element, being solid, introverted and heavy. On the black mirror, the magician will write about a lack of toughness, lack of patience, and lack of perseverance, and every time he manifests a lack of any of these virtues he is to write it down until there are no such manifestations taking place. Mastering the three subordinate virtues is easier than it might appear, for mastering but one of them will offer the keys to mastering the others. When they are under the magician's dominion and he is rewarded with an unshakable will, he is to master the asana of volition, which is to be found by himself or shown to him by the personified power of unshakable will.

Air Principle: Knowing
Root Virtue Supreme wisdom
Subordinate Virtues: Diligence, assiduity and mastery of the laws

The magician is to know the laws and come to master them with assiduity and diligence. This will lead him to supreme wisdom. The black mirror is for lack of diligence, lack of assiduity, and failure in applying the laws. The subordinate virtues are all of the air, which is expansive, extroverted and light. The asana of knowing is to be applied once wisdom is achieved. On the virtues that follow we will refrain from repeating this information.

Water Principle: Daring
Root Virtue: Disclosing mystery
Subordinate Virtues: Courage and indifference to others' opinions and firmness

Only by being courageous, firm in his objectives and indifferent to others' opinions will the magician be able to access the inner mysteries, and once tapping into them, he will continue to explore them with volition, just like a holy task or an act of priesthood. For this reason, it may have been that the Holy Grail was attributed as the sacred weapon of the water element. From what has been previously given, the magician knows how to operate the black mirror, it being the lack of these qualities, and also when to discover and practice the asana of daring.[14]

The magician gains an understanding of how to operate the black soul mirror, because of the lack of these qualities, and also when to discover and practise the asana of daring. Courage is of the fire and it is expansive, introverted and hot. Indifference to others' opinions is free and of the air. Firmness combines aspects of the earth and of the fire. The root virtue, being of the water, is malleable, extroverted and cold.

Earth Principle: Silence
Root Virtue: Connection to the Supreme Source
Subordinate Virtues: Power, being reticent and discrete

---

[14] As mentioned previously, If the magician is working through intuition the figures of imagination built by him from the personification of the powers will answer and show him the asana, but if he is using reason he is to research bodily postures and their symbolism and he is to apply them.

Being reticent is to be mastered first, for it will give access to power management, and power management is the highest nature of power itself. Finally, the magician is to check if he is manifesting enough power, for if he isn't, this is a sign that discretion isn't being applied properly. The enemies of discretion on the black mirror are bragging, which is the lack of discretion, and segregation, which is its excess. The power lies in every element. Being reticent and discreet is a trait of the earth element. Segregation is of the earth element and bragging of the air element. The inertia of the earth element can be used against itself so that, for instance, inert segregation would then start surrendering into a processable emotion. Or, likewise, the airy looseness of bragging can be locked down and densified into an emotion behind it, by imposing on its watery aspects, so that the healing process can begin.

Now, each time the magician masters a virtue, not once having acted against it during the course of a week or twenty-eight days, he is to inscribe a symbolic representation of it in a weapon and, gathering all his senses, he is to fix his concentration on the virtue while gazing continually at the symbol until a mist a light, or a misty light starts surrounding it. The attributions are as follows:

Sword

The pommel, grip and quillion (cross guard) are to be inscribed and charged with the three subordinate virtues, and the blade with an unshakable will.

Wand

The handle is inscribed and charged with the mastery of the laws, a ring is inserted in the rod with the symbol of assiduity, and another with the symbol of diligence and they are charged accordingly. The edge of the rod, wand or staff, should have a talismanic item, be it a crystal, a feather, a bone or a bell, and it is to be inscribed with a visual for supreme wisdom and charged accordingly. The magician should be able to remove the talismanic item when needed, for later he will learn how to handle the staff through martial or artistic disciplines, and he will not want to have the talisman in danger of falling or breaking against something.

Cup

Firmness is to be at the base, indifference to others' opinions and courage at the sides, and the virtue of disclosing mystery on the inside.

Pentacle

A pentagram inside a circle is to be built on a circular piece of wood, the circle should contain discretion, the centre of the pentagram is to contain the power, and the upper triangle of the pentagram is to represent a connection with the supreme source.

Further guidance on the attitude in which the magician should handle the instruments or build them himself can be consulted in *The Practice of Magical Evocation* by Franz Bardon. But in any case, they will help in sealing away the opposites of these powers and solidifying the magician's virtues, making them impermeable to distractions. The weapons will feel alive and when the magician touches them with purity and respect he will be immediately connected to divine authority and magical equilibrium.

tep 6

Gaming of the Unicorn

It is time for the magician to extend his powers of concentration and imagination. He will treat each principle as a realm in itself. He will have, therefore, the realm of volition, the realm of knowing, the realm of daring, and the realm of silence. First, he will imagine objects in each realm, and fix his imagination and concentration, uniting the effects of the sensorial organs, auditory organs, olfactory organs, vision and taste, so that these objects will stand as if they are really in the room. Five minutes should be practised holding the imagination to each object. Different objects evoke different senses. Some may be censers with burning incense, some may be musical in nature, some may be organic, cold or warm to the touch, and some may be food or drinks. Next, a person corresponding to the realm of the object should be imagined while handling the object. Then the magician is to imagine the nature, natural elements, colours, light intensities, forms, atmosphere and landscape of that realm where the person is handling the instrument. A sign of success is that such worlds and realms become absolutely natural to the magician and standing in them for five minutes stops being a burden to the magician's vitality. When this is done, he can move and explore in his mind, touching the plasticity of everything, letting nothing skip his powers of observation, such as sounds, spirits, fauna, flora, and the inhabitants of each realm and their voices and movements. The root virtues may be easily seen roaming around like kings, governors and so on, and the subordinate virtues as princes or something analogous.

Next, the magician will be able to open his eyes and evoke such realms, having his physical surroundings disappear to give them a place. Let him interact. When five minutes is effortless in any case and the magician has known well each of the realms, he may move on.

Taming of the Pegasus

It is time for the magician to imagine, in the asana of volition and holding his sword near, that the whole universe is made of unshakable will and that it lives in the form of an endless red hot fire expanding in all directions and leaving nothing else. On the other hand, the magician's body, physical and astral, is to be imagined as an empty vessel. Through the whole body and the nose, and breathing deeply but naturally, the magician inhales this fiery unshakable will until his body feels red hot like an ember. The magician can use his string of mala beads to count the inhalations, so that, after he is done, he exhales the element as many times as he has inhaled it.

The same applies to supreme wisdom, which is to be imagined fully inhabiting a universe solely made of blue winds. At the asana of knowing and holding the wand near, the magician breathes it in. The first sign of success is that the magician starts to feel like a balloon. At the second sign, he starts to feel extremely light, and finally, it appears to him that his body has disappeared. Then he breathes the element out, accordingly.

Now he works under a new concept, the unshakable will of supreme wisdom so that where wisdom was passive, it now becomes active, and where the will was limitless, it now becomes bound and tempered by wisdom. While this is the mental sensation, the astral sensation is that of a fiery lightness, and the physical body feels like a fire balloon. The colour is purple. There is no asana to this practice, it is sufficient that the body remains alert and relaxed, and that the sword and the wand are near.

Next, comes the asana of daring, and breathing disclosure of mystery in its massive body of greenish-blue water, so massive that the whole universe is made of it. The body becomes cold, and with continuous practice, it begins to feel like an ice lump. The cup is to be kept near. As always, the magician should exhale the element back.

At the asana of silence and having the pentacle around him he is to breathe in his connection with the source, with all his bodies being vacant to receive the body of the source. He imagines the world to be made of the density and gravity of the supreme source, and that it is filling his own body with each inhalation. The density is of a yellow oscillation, the gravity is grey, and the supreme source black, so that the fluid the magician is breathing in is a dynamic vibration of the three colours flowing inside each other. A sign of success is that the body starts to paralyse. Another sign of success is that it feels to the magician as if it has turned into lead.

The fluid to follow is that of the unveiled mystery of the supreme source. There is not much that can be said about it except that it is both an extremely personal subject and an extremely universal one. It is attained through gnosis and it is untransmittable except through initiation. The astral feeling is that of a density in the cold around which gravity moves. The universe is to become like that fluid and to be breathed into the vacant body, which is to become as solid and heavy as lead and as cold as ice. The colours are yellow-green flowing with dark forest green and green-grey. No specific asana is required. The magical weapons are the cup and the pentacle.

Finally, the magician is, again, to breathe in the unveiled mystery of the supreme source and, once it is entirely fused with his astral and physical bodies and the concept is well fixed on his mental body, so that he has become the principal himself, he breathes in the unshakable will of supreme wisdom so that it goes inside the unveiled mystery of the supreme source and the magician feels the exterior of his body to be made of an icy lump of heavy lead and the interior feels similar to a fire balloon. There is no specific asana, and a sword, wand, cup and pentacle should form a cross around the magician.

Finally, the magician is to repeat each fluid imbued with the virtue to the extent that, once he has achieved the final signs of success, he keeps on accumulating the element until the whole room is shining and vibrating with it. Then, he is to release the element and its tension, allowing the virtue to remain alone.

Physical Mirror and Taming of the Horse

To the practice of Chi Kung, Tai Chi and Kung Fu, the magician is to add five more minutes of basic Yoga, deepening it only when and if it feels natural to him. Alternatively, he is to give each day of the week to one of these practices, dedicating the fifth to the practice of the asanas of the four hermetic principles. At the weekend, he is to rest.

Only when the magician has completely fixed and mastered the four hermetic principles is he to pass on to step 7.

Step 7

Taming of the Unicorn

At this stage, the magician is faced again with a large soul mirror based on *The Key to True Kabbalah*[15] by Franz Bardon. The idea here is that the magician utilises the active qualities, dependent on his efforts, to conquer the passive qualities. Every time the magician engages in something that goes against the passive quality, he is to note it down in his magical diary. And only after three to seven days of no inner engagement with anything that contradicts the quality he is aiming at, may he proceed to the following letter[16].

---

[15] Franz Bardon, *The Key to the True Quabbalah* (Germany: Dieter Rüggeberg/Wuppertal, 1971).

[16] Such letters are not to be intoned kabbalistically as in the *Key to True Quabbalah*. Instead, in order to work Bardon's cosmic letters, we are using the technique of the soul mirror as we have accustomed our reader. It suffices for the practitioner to follow the instructions attentively as they are being given.

Fire Element

Letter	Active Quality	Passive Quality	Sign of Success
C	Self-Spiritualisation	Divine Ideas	When the magician has no thought that he is not connected to the divine.
D	Creativity	Ego-consciousness in all elemental analogies	When the magician has no thought that is not self-conscious.
H	Power of the Word	Understanding of Divine Providence	There is a special way in which to work this letter.
K	Standing pure and above all things	Faith	When the magician has no thought that is not faithful.
S	Contact with divine Spirit	Prophecy	As with the H letter, there is a special way of working the S. The magician is to take all phenomena as a direct conversation between himself and the divine spirit, and every time the magician loses connection, he writes it down in the magical diary. A sign of success is that he loses his connection less and less until such loss stops manifesting for a whole week. The second sign of success is that the divine spirit starts communicating to him that which is to be. The third sign of success is that he becomes a witness to the prophecy that was given to him. We leave it to the magician's decision to stay with the first sign of success or to go all the way until the third before moving on.

Sh	Highest enlightenment	Spiritual ecstasy	When the magician has trained his mind to make a perception of the fire that turns everything it touches into the light, he attains spiritual ecstasy. If the magician feels that he has lost this kind of grace, he is to write it down and restart.
T	Divine inspiration	Invention	Focusing on divine inspiration the magician is to keep his inventive spirit throughout his days. If ever he feels blocked in his inventive capacities, he is to write it down together with why and how this impediment takes place.

Air Element

Letter	Active Quality	Passive Quality	Sign of Success
A	Highest wisdom	High intelligence	Wisdom is the focus of the mind and its source of inspiration; intelligence is the effect. If ever the magician notices that he is hopelessly lacking in intellectual capacity or reasoning, no matter what the challenge is, he is to write it down and begin again.
L	Virtue	Morality	Immoral thoughts are hindrances to the progress of the magician in the given context. When no immoral thoughts or actions emerge, the magician is ready to move on.
Z	Cognition	Talent	Cognition is not only a process but also an action, that of acquiring knowledge and understanding through thought, experience and the senses

Water Element

Letter	Active Quality	Passive Quality	Sign of Success
G	Grace	Peacefulness	The magician may easily measure his failures by his loss of peace. Grace will be his discipline.
Ch	Clarity	Oratory skills	The magician may easily measure his failures when, while making use of language, he is unable to come clear.
J	Love	Ecstasy	The magician should think of love through a cosmic filter so that nothing will stain it. Through constant concentration on such love, is he to come to ecstasy. It is by the continuity of these ecstasies of love that he may measure his success.
M	Fluidity	Clear feelings and acute sensations	The magician may easily measure his failures by when he loses the purity of his feelings and of his senses. If this is not occurring, he obtains his first sign of success, the second being a natural increase of empathy.
N	Happiness	Unison of emotion and intellect	The magician may easily measure his failures by divisions and conflicts between emotion and intellect. Happiness and delight can and may be practised, and although people regard it as a passive principle it is an active principle and a holy spiritual discipline; it forgets the problems of the mind, the soul and the body in order to engage in existence.

| W | Intuition | Mediumistic abilities | Intuition must be practised through a cosmic filter, that is, it is not an intuition about things and attached to them, but over things and detached from them. Mastering these virtues will teach much to the magician, for if he loses balance and lets his intuition be influenced by the phenomenal world he will be working with delusions in terms of mediumistic faculties, which, with his trained mind, he can easily unmask and dissipate. His mediumistic explorations should be of a universal nature. When they are perfectly refined and accurate, there is success. |

Earth Element

Letter	Active Qualities	Passive Qualities	Sign of Success
B	Cognition of polarity	Influence over fate	The magician's focus, on all matters, is towards the understanding of polarity, plus and minus and the chain of all things, and of how, in terms of polarity, each thing influences the other. By moulding his perception tirelessly in such a way, he starts to have a clear idea of the causes and effects of all things. He is to avail it to his or another's benefit, and when he fails in his calculations he is to start again.
F	Harmony	Unification of faculties	It is by the dominion over the B that the magician will come to perfectly understand the legality. Once he is used to it, it presents itself immediately, no matter what is being analysed as the harmony of the thing observed. That sense of harmony at all times is the focus of the magician. The sign of success is when the magician finds and determines the perfect harmony between will, thought, emotion and his own identity acting and existing according to the harmony mentioned. Major interferences to this process are to be written down and the magician should start from zero, but this time with increased experience.

I	Evolution	Memory	The magician is to shape his perception of the world to a sense of evolution and progression. Evolution is the tissue uniting all things in space so that the disposition of anything is in accordance to how it may evolve in relation to the other things and also how it can make them evolve. Later, he shifts it to his relation with time on an individual level, so that the events of his daily life will start to bring in insights relating to his memories. If the magician finds that his memory is in high performance for three to seven consecutive days, and not failing him even in the most mundane matters, he may move on.
O	Justice	Judgement	The magician may easily measure his failures by bad judgements on his part. His mind is focused on justice, but if he is practising bad judgements, he is still synchronising with the object of his concentration.
P	Spiritualisation	Devotion	This letter is an extraversion of the C. The magician's focus will be on spiritualising the many aspects of the outside world with which he interacts and if he finds that his devotion towards these things is lacking, neither spiritualisation nor devotion has been stabilised. With repetition, these virtues will become concentrated and make it easier for the magician to advance in his training.
R	Independence	Maturity	While the magician is striving to act independently and from an original place of independence in all instances, he should be checking with diligence his lack of maturity, for without maturity independence can never be real.

Ae	Transformation	Seeing through all thoughts, desires and wishes	While the magician works to see how anything exists inside that on which it may become, thoughts, desires and wishes cease to trick him in any way. If under this oath, he still finds himself being surprised by others and by the events of life, he is not ready to advance.

Taming of the Pegasus

It is time for the magician to vitalise his organs and bodily parts with the corresponding virtues and their outpouring of fluids. In order to do that he is to breathe in, as he has done previously, but through different regions of the body. He starts by totally infusing an organ or a body part and later expands the energy so that it enlivens the whole body, that being the time when the signs of success are to manifest. Then, as before, he releases and dissipates the astral saturation, leaving only the virtue or quality. Remember that all the colours we will give to the fiery letters are to have a hot and expansive sensation to them, the oscillations of air are to be light and lifting, the oscillations of water are to be of a burning cold, and the colour oscillations of the earth are to feel dense and heavy.

Fire Element - Through the Breath

Letter	Instruction	Sign of Success
C	He breathes in self spiritualised divine ideas into the stomach under a vermillion colour oscillation, after which he expands it to the whole body.	When the magician finds out that he can modify his astral aura at will with this method, he has succeeded.
D	The magician breathes in the creativity of the ego consciousness into the right ear in a dark blue colour, after which he expands it to the whole body.	Erotic arousal is a sign that the fluid has been properly densified.
H	The magician is to breathe in the Word of Divine Providence to the right arm, under a silver violet oscillation, after which he expands it to the whole body.	When, by this impregnation, the magician is able to influence fate, he has succeeded.
K	The magician is to breathe in unshakable faith to his left ear under the silver-blue light oscillation, after which he expands it to the whole body.	When the magician is inflamed by ecstatic courage.
S	The magician is to breathe in the divine spirit of prophecy to his gall bladder under the purple oscillation, after which he expands it to the whole body.	Activation of clairvoyant abilities.
Sh	The magician is to breathe in enlightened ecstasy to his head under the red oscillation, after which he expands it to the whole body.	A strong surge of will-power.
T	The magician breathes in the spirit of divine invention to the right kidney under the dark brown oscillation, after which he expands it to the whole body.	The magician finds out that, during his trance, he has perfect control of his astral surroundings and of the atmosphere of the room.

The Air Element - Through the Breath

Letter	Instruction	Sign of Success
A	The magician is to breathe in the intelligence of wisdom into his lungs and breasts under the light blue oscillation, after which he expands it to the whole body.	A state of eloquence and poetic inspiration.
L	The magician is to breathe in moral virtue into the spleen under a dark green oscillation, after which he expands it to the whole body.	A natural accumulation of astral light.
Z	The magician is to breathe in the talents of cognition into the heart under the lemon yellow oscillation, after which he expands it to the whole body.	Artistic inspiration.

The Water Element - Through the Breath

Letter	Instruction	Sign of Success
G	The magician is to breathe in graceful peace into the left eye under the grass green oscillation, after which he expands it to the whole body.	A deep feeling of happiness and satisfaction.
Ch	The magician is to breathe in articulated or dynamic clarity into the left leg under the violet colour oscillation, after which he expands it to the whole body.	An acute instinct for rhythm or a sharp perception of rhythm.
J	The magician is to breathe ecstatic love into the diaphragm under the dark opal oscillation, after which he expands it to the whole body.	Sympathetic feelings and perceptions.
M	The magician is to breathe in the fluidity of feelings and sensations into the abdomen under the blue-green oscillation, after which he expands it to the whole body.	The feeling is the same as when the magician mastered the accumulation of the water element.
N	The magician breathes in the happiness of mind and soul into the liver under a flesh red oscillation, after which he expands it to the whole body.	Activation of the will to live.
W	The magician breathes in mediumistic intuition into the abdomen under the lilac oscillation, after which he expands it to the whole body.	Manifestations of clairaudience or of dense mystical feelings.

The Earth Element - Through the Breath

Letters	Instruction	Signs of Success
B	The magician breathes in the power of polarity over fate, driving it into the right eye under the violet oscillation, after which he expands it to the whole body.	A sharp intuition.
F	The magician breathes in the harmony between all powers into the left hand under the light green oscillation, after which he expands it to the whole body.	Clear access to abstract ideas in their purest state.
I	The magician breathes in the evolution of memory into the left kidney under an opal oscillation, after which he expands it to the whole body.	Acute perception of all life in his body.
O	The magician is to breathe in the harmony of justice into the throat, thymus and larynx on an aquamarine colour, after which he expands it to the whole body	A deep sense of justice and emotional contentment.
P	The magician is to breathe in spiritual devotion into the right nostril in a grey colour, after which he expands it to the whole body.	Emotional purity, a clear sense of beauty.
R	The magician breathes in mature independence into the left nostril with a golden colour, after which he expands it to the whole body.	A regained feeling of ingenuity.
Ae	The magician breathes in the feeling of seeing through all transformations, this feeling being imbued with the sensory feeling of the earth element. He breathes on a dark brown colour into the coccyx and later expands it through the whole body	A feeling of self-satisfaction, complete independence and freedom.

There are other letters for which the magician is not yet ready, but he should enliven the corresponding body parts just the same, making use of the so-called water from the moon[17], the fluid/wish of vitality itself. The body parts are the spine, the solar plexus, the adrenals and the gonads. He should also keep in mind the right leg and the left and right foot[18]. The water of the moon can be used in any part of the body and is able to restitute it and heal it.

Optionally, the magician can, at this point, try to reach a deeper state of magical equilibrium. He will do it by inhaling the letters and the vital fluids until all the organs and body parts are filled. Then he breathes in through his whole body the water from the moon. This will create a dynamo where all the letters - with all their faculties - and vital fluids expand to the whole body simultaneously. The effect will be very similar to the formulation of Yod-Heh-Vav-Heh but we, elaborating no further, will leave the magician to be the judge of such things.

Taming of the Horse

The magician is to take long walks whenever possible, for it will help him obtain clarity on all fields and keep his channels of introspection clear.

---

[17] This is the water of life, the aqua vita of the alchemists and the soma of the Hindus. It reflects cosmic principle on a higher level and the very fluid of vitality and fertility on a lower level, as expressed in the Chandogya Upanishad, "From the scattered cloud proceeds condensed or raining cloud, which rains. From that proceeds rice, corn, annuals, trees, sesame, lentils and the like. Now, verily it is difficult to descend therefrom. Those who eat rice and procreate, become manifold."

[18] "(...) the soul ascends to the moon, which is called the ship of the Water of Life (navis vitalium aquarum). It is made of good water (ex bona aqua) or, according to a Parthian fragment, of wind and immortal water. There, or just below the moon in the Milky Way, which was regarded as the Column of Glory or the Perfect Man, the soul was to receive the "baptism of the gods." The Column of Glory was closely related to Jesus." (The Rediscovery of Gnosticism, Bentley Layton, 1981).

Step 8

Taming of the Unicorn

At this stage, the magician is to test his progress by elaborating upon three simple mirrors.

Mental Mirror
Strong Willpower / Weak Willpower
Great Resistance / Weak Resistance
Good Memory / Bad Memory
Keen Observation / Poor Observation
Clear Intellect / Murky Intellect

Astral Mirror
Calm / Anxiety
Steady / Unstable

Material Mirror
Healthy / Unhealthy
Good Shape / Bad Shape
Rejuvenated / Depleted

He will test his white mirror against his black mirror, writing down, at the end of the day, how many times he has engaged with the qualities of the white mirror and how many times he came to engage or has manifested the defects from the black mirror. He is to also divide the occasions by three levels of intensity. Most probably, at this stage, the black mirror will not pose an obstacle at all. Also, if the magician suffers from some incurable sickness or disability he may not be as healthy as those unmolested by sickness, but he will think of the word healthy as healthier. The same applies to other exceptions.

Taming of the Pegasus

Bardon[19] writes,

Through pulmonary and pore breathing of your entire body, you inhale vital force, pressing it with all your imagination into your whole body, so that it, as it were, becomes dynamically radiant. Your body is something like radiant energy, the focus or let me say, an individual sun. With every inhaling you enforce the compressed vital power as well as the radiant energy, and fill the room you live in. With the aid of this radiant power, the room must be literally sunlit.

and he adds that the magician can, by the strength of his imagination, give back the vital virtue that has been accumulated by breathing it out, thus leaving the force of light and radiation in the room.

Concerning objects and biomagnetism, he writes that one might charge any object with the wish to bless the person wearing it with fortune and success. The vital virtue can be fixed in the object via imagination and concentrated wish, and it can be timed so that the force remains forever in it, drawing further and further from the universe as this person wears the object. Another option given by Franz Bardon is that the object is loaded for a short time only, the power dispersing as soon as the aimed purpose is attained. A third possibility, universal loading, includes in the technique the concentrated wish that as long as the object exists the blessing is given.

Such universal loadings performed by an adept will keep their virtues and their effects for centuries.[20]

It is time for the magician to apply such methods to his conquered virtues, having them self-maintaining at each hour of each day.

To this effect, he should choose a ring to charge with the desire and effect of having strong willpower, his shoes he is to charge with the desire and effect of having great resistance, and his clock or wrist mala with the desire of having a good memory, his glasses or sunglasses with the wish of having the faculty of keen observation, and his hat with the desire of

---

[19] Franz Bardon, *Initiation into Hermetics* (Germany: Rüggeberg-Verlag, 1993), 86.

[20] Franz Bardon, *Initiation into Hermetics* (Germany: Rüggeberg-Verlag, 1993), 89.

having a clear intellect. He is to set in the timing and constant renewal of the blessings, also, the radiation of the objects should extend to about one yard around the objects. Again, let him remember that he can program an object to bless someone else with the same properties, depending on the extension of his imagination. He is to act as in Bardon's description above, but his hands will be placed above the objects and the radiation will flow from them into the objects, fixing itself.

Now he will practise with the impregnation of spaces, also commanding the astral light to renew itself at every hour of every day according to the direction of his wishes. In his bedroom, he should install peace, in his living room, steadiness. The area should be so firmly blessed that the magician is able to see the astral oscillations and impregnations with his naked eye, which a third person, even if untrained, is likely to do as well.

Next, the magician will use these methods to heal himself and others, imbuing the vital power with health, the feeling of being in good shape and with rejuvenation. He has to concentrate the fluid on his whole body – physical, astral and mental – or on a particular region of the body that is being afflicted. If he is healing another, he has to accumulate the fluid of health, good shape or rejuvenation, or all three together, to the extent that it radiates ten yards around him, then he projects into the patient by imposing on him his hands, as he did to objects, until the fluid flows for about one yard around the patient. Again, the fluid is to be programmed so that it renews itself constantly until it achieves the realisation of its mission.

Gaming of the Horse

The magician is to learn the Shaolin basic staff techniques, practising with his magical staff if possible. This practice is important to make the magician feel the wand is an extension of his body. Also, such practice of handling an outside tool with inner grace and equilibrium will put the magician in the place of exercising the qualities of the staff, its wisdom being the outpouring of spiritual will.

Taming of the Unicorn

At this time the magician will transfer his consciousness to his magical tools concerning the four hermetic principles: the sword, the staff, the cup and the pentacle.

About this, Bardon[21] writes that the magician, in his asana, is to fix his eyes on the object and inculcate in his or her mind the shape, colour and size of it. The magician feels that he or she is the object, adapting all its properties and unable to abandon his spot except by outside influences. Concentrating, the magician, at this point, regards his surroundings from inside the object and remains in its shape, size and quality for at least five uninterrupted minutes.

Now, the magician will transfer his consciousness to the fire poppy, the flower of willpower; to the sage plant, the plant of wisdom; to the apple, the fruit of mystery unveiled and to the olive tree, the tree of connection with the divine source.

Next in line come the animals, first lying still and then moving in their regular activities. Remember that the magician needs to imagine with all plasticity these animals, and needs not to be near them. We will want to be working with the animals of the four hermetic principles. The tiger, for instance, is an animal of willpower. The owl is considered the bird of wisdom. The serpent is considered to be the reptile of mystery. For the connection to the supreme source, the magician will use the imaginary sphinx, with the body of the lion, a human head and wings. Additionally, he is to try the unicorn as the source of divine mental concentration, the pegasus as the divine freedom of the soul, and the horse as the animal representing the endurance of the body.

[21] Franz Bardon, *Initiation into Hermetics* (Germany: Rüggeberg-Verlag, 1993), 95.

On transferring one's consciousness to animals, Bardon[22] states,

Adepts who have been practising this exercise for years are able to understand any animal and handle it by their will power.

Then without discrimination of age and sex, the magician will search the acquaintances of people he considers to have a great amount of volition, knowledge, silence, or who are especially daring. He is to transfer his consciousness to them and study these characteristics in action. Later, he is to try persons that represent the mastering of these qualities. For instance, Aleister Crowley is known for having become addicted to a myriad of drugs intently, in order to prove his willpower in fighting them. While this wasn't a complete success without some help, in the end, he surely went far enough to prove his point. He became the head of most of the magical orders of his time with the intent of making their secrets known. He can be set as an example of volition. But also, among many other things, he made himself known as a bisexual, assumed to himself the place of the prophet of a new age using the name of the Beast 666, became a mountaineer champion and was certainly a master at the art of daring. Omraam Aivahnov was an adept, especially talented in the oral art of spoken wisdom. The adept Kenneth Grant went through great pains to disclose the mystery. Franz Bardon is a great master of all four principles, but he has a greater deal of silence and discretion than most, and while he speaks plainly, he speaks with silence and discretion.

Finally, the magician is to go back to the personifications of his sublimated instincts, and he is to transfer into them his consciousness and explore their realms. Bardon closes the topic of the transplant of consciousness as follows:

The exercise is ended if you manage to transplant your consciousness for at least five minutes into the imaginary bodies. The longer the spell of this achievement, the more profitable it will become.[23]

---

[22] Franz Bardon, *Initiation into Hermetics* (Germany: Rüggeberg-Verlag, 1993), 96.

[23] Franz Bardon, *Initiation into Hermetics* (Germany: Rüggeberg-Verlag, 1993), 97.

Taming of the Pegasus

It is time for the magician to learn how to breathe out or disperse the elemental accumulation of certain virtues through the whole body in a single effort, without having to exhale more than once. But first, he will breathe in the virtue of a connection with the supreme source as a gravitational pull at the limbs, genitals and the base of the spine. He starts by breathing through the whole body and then compresses it to this region, so that, now being limited to a smaller area, it intensifies. He then, after dissipating the fluid at once, breathes in the virtue of disclosing mystery in the body of water, compressing it in the abdominal region, then supreme wisdom under the sensory stimulations of air, in the same way, and compresses it at the chest. He finally proceeds to unshakable will under the condensation of fire He is not to forget the organs attached to these areas. Later, when he is used to it, he is to do all four regions accordingly but simultaneously. This practice will bring the magician back to balance at any time. It is useful if, to each accumulation, the magician adds the proper asana: the asana of volition, the asana of knowing, the asana of daring, and the asana of keeping silence.

The magician is also to measure his success by building a black mirror and keeping it in check. The black mirror should contain as negative aspects "losing centre", "illness", and "being ill influenced".

In the white mirror, he will search for manifestations of "mental clarity", "emotional strength", "magical faculties", "universal intuition", and "refined senses".

Taming of the Horse

It is time for the magician to work with rituals. To this end, he has acquired a variety of tools. For once, the talismans of his virtues such as the coins, the symbols of his virtues, and the tools such as the cup, the sword, the staff and the pentacle, but also the hat, the glasses, the wrist mala, the necklace mala, the ring and his magical shoes. Additionally, he has mastered the asanas and gestures of Qigong, Tai Chi, Yoga and Kung Fu. We will leave yoga and the martial arts to the knowledge of the magician, as he has advanced freely in these disciplines. The coins can be used to prepare the space and form a circle so that the magician feels rewarded by his virtues and devas. The symbols of the virtues can be drawn in the air accompanied by vital accumulation. The cup, sword, staff and pentacle can function as the coins but with a more universal quality, also the wand can be used, by now, to trace symbols, to bless and to perform gestures. If the magician has worked with the remaining objects such as the ring, the hat, and so on, they have become self-explanatory, but the idea is that the magician is able to perform the ritual with as few distractions as possible and from the purest view. The preparation of the tools is as a meditation that will align him with his sacred self; it will build the magician's own temple. The asanas should be trained with the vital accumulation of the corresponding virtues and anchor or transplant of consciousness to the personified virtues, to the extent that through repetition of the asanas accumulation and consciousness transference takes place automatically. Bypassing from one asana to another the magician is able to form sequences of accumulation and radiation according to different intentions.

Another important aspect is the mudras. About them, Bardon writes the following:

> In conformity with the elements, they are using the analogy of the five fingers by imputing the forefinger to fire, the thumb to the water, the middle finger to the akasha, the ring-finger to the earth and the little finger to the air. The right hand represents the positive elements and the left one the negative elements. May this small example be sufficient.[24]

But it is important that the magician practises accumulation in the whole body and then concentrates the impregnated vital fluids in the

---

[24] Franz Bardon, *Initiation into Hermetics* (Germany: Rüggeberg-Verlag, 1993), 102.

71

fingers. In the context of the present work, fire is being expressed and directed by unshakable will, water by the virtue of disclosing mystery, earth by connection to the supreme source, and air by supreme wisdom, while the akasha has been used as neutral vital power so far. If the magician is accumulating the elemental virtues in the fingers of his right hand, he can use the fingers of the left hand as a compliment. For instance, a will that makes the world shake, the protective and enshrouding properties of mystery, supreme freedom, and the supreme actions of the source. The middle finger can concede vital power in one hand and suck vital power with another. The important thing is that the fingers are so strongly charged that their gestures immediately impregnate time, space, objects and beings according to the ideals and virtues of the magician.

To come to the best of his abilities, the magician is to test his soul mirror again before compromising himself. He will test it for "assurance", "self-confidence", "self-reliance" and "unshakable faith".

Step 10

Taming of the Unicorn

Another extra mirror is waiting in the wings. The magician will write Inner Light, and under that section, he will add enlightenment, cognition, experience and intuition. Every time he counters his enlightenment or intuition, he is to make a note, and every day he is also to write down how it was that he has advanced in cognition and experience. If the table of cognition and experience is empty at the end of the day, he must restart. If enlightenment and intuition have been given a mark, on that day the magician must restart as well. If the magician completes five days without having to restart, he may move on.

Now he will write in "Absolute Power", and under it, he is to write the subordinate virtues of will, power and strength. If he manifests weakness or lack of power he is to mark under "strength" and "power". If he acts against his will he is to do the same under the section of will. At each mark, the tables restart. Five days will come to pass with no mark, after which the magician continues.

Next, comes "absolute authority", and under it, the magician writes "superiority" and "victory". It is by mastering superiority that he may come to victory. If at any time, any power or being can subdue the magician, the magician cannot proceed and he must start counting the days from the start. If any mood gets the better of him and makes him obedient, he is to proceed in the same manner.

Then, "Spiritual Perfection". This quality should have the subordinate virtues of dignity and authority. The dignity square is to be marked whenever the magician engages with things opposing dignity, the authority square by positive manifestations of authority. The magician will understand that the more he preserves dignity the more he will manifest true authority.

We will work now under the attribute of "Absolute Purity of All Ideas". This volt is achieved by the virtue of having "purity of soul" and the power of "protection". These two are the subordinate qualities, with which the magician will work directly. At any time when the magician is violating the purity of his soul he will mark the corresponding square, and every time that he notices he is being protected, he is to mark the square of "protection", so that one works with negative confessions and the other with positive confessions. The magician will understand that the more he protects the purity of his soul the more he will be protected as a whole, and when this state becomes continuous, he achieves the uninterrupted purity of all ideas.

On to the attribute of "magical equilibrium", with "dominion over the elements" as the active subordinate and "balance" as the passive. The passive should suffer from negative confessions and the active form positive confessions.

Accordingly, we will work with the attribute of "divine blood". Under it, we are to assign "wisdom", "power" and "vitality". The magician uses negative confessions every time he contradicts wisdom as well as every time he acts against his vital source and his vitality. At the same time, he writes down his manifestations of true power, so that he may come to notice that true power is a conjunction of wisdom and life and that when power, wisdom and life act together, they manifest the strength of the divine blood.

Finally, work must be done towards "absolute power". It must be measured by two root virtues or qualities, "intellectual power" and "psychic power". The magician is to keep track of his success concerning intellectual power by never contradicting a positive attitude, and psychic power must be measured by the number of manifestations of maturity.

Taming of the Pegasus

It is time to give each of these qualities an object and to charge them from a new point of view – the depth point. How one is to practise such disciplines is given by Bardon, who writes that the magician should fix his eyes on the object, close them and transfer his consciousness to its centre. The transplantation of consciousness has the magician forget his body, feeling as small as an atom. Afterwards, the dimension and shape of the object is to be seized from the depth point and the magician's

75

consciousness keeps shrinking until the width and circumference of the object represents the universe. For as long as possible, the magician holds onto this feeling. Upon success, he or she recognizes the material and mental structures of the chosen objects, obtaining the faculty to influence them from the nucleus and to load them magically at will.

- The magician will practise with a lamp, and charge it with Inner Light.
- The magician will practise with his staff, and charge it with Absolute Power.
- The magician will practise with his sword, and charge it with Absolute Victory.
- The magician will practise with his hat, and charge it with Spiritual Perfection.
- The magician will practise with a robe, and charge it with absolute purity of all ideas.
- The magician will practise with a belt, and charge it with magical equilibrium.
- The magician will practise with his cup, and charge it with the idea of the divine blood.
- Finally, the magician is to practise with his pentacle and charge it with the idea of supreme dominion.

When the magician has become proficient at charging the tools inwardly, he is to charge them outwardly by accumulating the fluids of the qualities mentioned above through the whole body and expelling them through the solar plexus in the form of a sphere. The sphere is to be imagined as a fiery sun of the quality, and with further accumulation, a small blue atmosphere impregnated with the quality is to cover it, then a spherical lump of ice in the same manner, and a sphere of clay, but the light of the sun still shining through the clay. The magician is to guide this sphere with his hands to each of the magical weapons and lodge it there, programming the sphere through its own depth point to create more and more of the same fluid and to preserve it by destroying opposite faults and influences.

Next, the magician is to draw a circle and, sitting at the centre, he is to lay the items throughout the circumference. Then he is to practise as he has done with the items and tools but on his own body. According to

Bardon[25], it can be done by the transplantation of one's consciousness into the middle of the body, it standing in the solar plexus or pit of the stomach. This zone holds the gravity of the body. The magician holds his consciousness in this centre for five minutes minimum and regards his body from that point. As the magician's consciousness becomes smaller, the bigger the circumference of his body becomes, until it reveals a whole universe. The magician incarnates the determining power in the centre of his own body. It is desirable that the magician is able to transfer himself at any time and situation into this depth-point, which is the akasha principle influencing the magician's own being. The exercise is extremely important because it introduces a genuine magical trance and is the beginning stage of cosmic consciousness.

At this stage and in this trance state, inside the circle, the magician will be able to work with more abstract and absolute ideas, ideas that are of an akashic nature. He is to enter an akashic trance and impregnate his structures with the ability of universal consciousness. He is to measure his success with a soul mirror that will have his control on a daily basis if his intuition is improving, together with his consciousness of the astral world and his capacities of condensing the fluids of the virtues or refining the fluids of his own soul. An additional practice may have the magician meditate in such a way that he is to separate relative truths, relative lies, personal truths, personal lies, and universal thoughts, until for five minutes at least only the universal thoughts remain.

When the above becomes natural, the magician is to enter an akashic trance and refine his structures so that they adopt an akashic nature and he should measure his success by verifying whether he is feeling constantly inspired, if consciousness transference becomes more and more natural and immediate to him and if his magical equilibrium is undisturbed.

At this time, the magician will apply the akashic trance in impregnating his structures with the original rhythm of life. Signs of success are that his mind becomes visionary, his soul will be able to feel the future, and he will be able to attract events from the past so that they renew themselves in the present.

Finally, the magician will impregnate his structures from the depth point with what we call the quintessence, that is, the fluidic ability to

---

25 Franz Bardon, *Initiation into Hermetics* (Germany: Rüggeberg-Verlag, 1993), 108.

perceive everything from the temporal depth point, while so far we have been using the spatial depth point. It translates into seeing the structure of things in all that they ever were, is and will be in time and being in the centre of such a whirlwind. Signs of success are that the magician is rendered capable of instantly transmuting vices and virtues together with emotions. His mind will become invisible and immortal to the manifest world, not being touched by manifestations but touching them and vivifying them.

After success is achieved, he is to do it the other way around, still inside the circle and surrounded by his magical weapons. He is to imagine a cosmic sphere around him made of the vitality of the quality and draw it from every way around him into his physical body, impregnating also his astral and mental structures until he and the quality become one and the same, but still, he must continue until the whole room is filled by his radiation. On a sensorial level, the qualities we have addressed are electromagnetic; they are both cold and hot and give the magician the sensation of levitation and gravity at the same time. For the ability of universal consciousness he will imagine the fluid to have a violet colour; for the refinement through the akasha, black; for the original rhythm of life, pink; for the quintessence, orange. When he is successful, he will run through the sequence again but without the vital qualities passing through his body. They are to come from the cosmos to impregnate the room directly. When the magician is done, he is to dissolve the condensations back into the cosmos through force of willpower and imagination.

Next, he is to draw the energy of each quality from the cosmic ball around him with the intention of accumulating it under the shape of a certain animated personification directly in the air. Again, his body is not to be a medium this time. Having become victorious over this practice and able to witness these personifications inhabiting the room with him, the magician will move on.

Taming of the Horse

The magician is to undergo a pilgrimage on which he shall test his mystical and magical skills.

tep 11

Taming of the Unicorn

The magician proceeds as was learned in order to become one with the cosmic virtues, but at this moment he is to give them expression through writing. Here the messages will be given as a sort of thinking aloud inside or outside the magician's own personality and all questions will be answered immediately. This is the method by which many holy books were written.

Additionally, the magician will meditate on his spirit, composed of fire as willpower, air as cognition, water as a feeling, and earth as consciousness. He will then meditate and reflect using all "four heads" simultaneously. This is done by first observing them and how and when they diverge, then fixing the attention of willpower, intellect, feeling and consciousness on the same subject, and finally, by having them articulate the same thoughts at the same time until, by the force of habit of keeping them in harmony, the magician uses all four heads simultaneously on his mundane and daily tasks.

Taming of the Pegasus

When this has become natural to the magician, he will add in a fifth head, that of the astral body, so that all the unified thinking between will, intellect, feeling and consciousness has a sensorial aspect densified in harmony with the four segments of the spirit. Later, we extend it to the body. About this, Bardon writes that when one is walking he or she is to think that it is the spirit that walks by moving the astral and material feet. The same applies to any moving part of the body. The practice is to last for at least ten continuous minutes, perfecting the so-called magical action.

The scholar will certainly understand now why magic rituals never show any success with persons who have not been initiated or who have not been trained in magic, because people like these do not own the capacity of executing the ritual magically.[26]

The magician will point out any feelings of dizziness or disturbances of balance as failures, and he may test his skills by performing massages which will feel to the patient like a miracle, for, with soul, body and mind, he will be massaging the body, the soul and the mind.

From here on the exercise is pretty much as taught by Bardon in Step 6 in IIH. The magician imagines that it is the spirit that sees through his eyes, that hears through his ears and touches through his body, with the help of the astral body. If the four segments of the spirit are solid to his comprehension, he will then start thinking with them in unison, and they are to think of sensing with the astral body, seeing, hearing and touching with the physical body.

If the magician has a firm hold of the practice, he may start studying the banishing and invoking pentagrams of the four elements, so that he will have four invoking pentagrams and four banishing pentagrams, which he will draw by having his spirit tracing them in the air with the help of the astral and physical body so that he is able to accumulate virtues or banish all opposition to virtues. This can be done by a single intention on all planes or consciously polarised, the latter rendering the magician a greater mastery of the matter. If the magician has privacy he may use his magical tools to draw the pentagrams and he may utter the words of the verbs. If, in a crowd, he may use his fingers with discretion. Below, we will give the table of correspondences to put the different segments working together through polarity while drawing the pentagrams.

[26] Franz Bardon, *Initiation into Hermetics* (Germany: Rüggeberg-Verlag, 1993), 124.
81

Pentagrams of Fire

Verb: To Will
Willpower: Absolute Victory
Intellect: Unshakable Willpower
Feeling: Expansion
Consciousness: Introversion
Astral Sensory: Heat
Sight: Red
Hearing: Very High Pitch
Touch: Burning
Tool: Sword

Pentagrams of Air

Verb: To Know
Willpower: Absolute Power
Intellect: Supreme Wisdom
Feeling: Light
Consciousness: Extroversion
Astral Sensory: Levitation
Sight: Blue
Hearing: High Pitch
Touch: Gaseous
Tool: Staff

Pentagrams of Water

Verb: To Dare
Willpower: Divine Blood
Intellect: Disclosing Mystery
Feeling: Fluidity
Consciousness: Extroversion
Astral Sensory: Ice-Cold
Sight: Blue-Green
Hearing: Low Pitch
Touch: Liquid
Tool: Cup

Pentagrams of Earth

Verb: To Keep Silence
Willpower: Supreme Dominion
Intellect: Connection to the Supreme Source
Feeling: Gravity
Consciousness: Introversion
Astral Sensory: Weight
Sight: Black/Brown
Hearing: Very Low Pitch
Touch: Solid
Tool: Pentacle

The magician is to practise with the pentagrams until they manifest their full effects automatically; just a portion of the effects is not enough here, the reason why the magician should write a soul mirror testing patience, endurance and tenacity in all matters so that he is not tricked into advancing because of the lack of any of those attributes.

Taming of the Horse

The magician should learn how to carefully manage the sword, no matter what discipline.

Step 12

The magician will go back to forming the animated shapes of the akashic virtues through saturation. The form should correspond to the virtue as well as, this time, to a job that the magician wishes to give to the virtue. A name should be given to this animated shape, being of the first letter of each word composing the imperative or present form that describes the objective of the newborn elemental. The contents of such a phrase should be impregnated on the shape through willpower and imagination. Finally, a time of expiration should be given to the being's life depending on his given mission, and the magician must be clear about this. The magician should then send the servitor on his mission, separating his own mental sphere from the servitor's mental sphere. From time to time, he is to call the being back and recharge it, but most of the time he is to forget about him entirely. If the mission connects, for instance, with someone else's mind, the magician sends the being into the mental sphere of the other person.

Beyond the obvious natural abilities of the servitor made out of universal consciousness, which can be defined by the subordinate virtues of that quality, this servitor can, for instance, be sent into a human or an animal mind either in the present, the past or the future, and transmit the thoughts of his host through clairaudience. He can as easily materialise or dematerialise situations.

- The servitors made out of akashic refinement, beyond the obvious, can act on the principle of the ether and on karmic modification.
- The servitors made out of the original rhythm of life, beyond the obvious, can install the law of harmony.
- The servitors made out of the plasmification of the quintessence, beyond the obvious, can become catalysts for evolution.

Once this is done, the magician is to go back to the personifications of the sublimated instincts. He is to fill the personification of sublimated hunger with the connection to the supreme source, programming it as he has done to the previous servitors, with the intent, this time, of having the servitor of Sublimated Hunger showing the magician his own astral larvae of fear, grief, sorrow, hatred and envy. About the astral larvae, Franz

Bardon[27] writes that it is created involuntarily in the mental sphere by intense physical excitement. The larva becomes stronger with frequent repetition of this physical excitement. Larvae are created involuntarily by any type of person, initiated or not. Yet, without attention being paid to the excitement, it fades and so does the larvae.

This means that in the mental sphere larvae are, at the expense of the mental matter of each individual, constantly being generated and dissipated. A strongly condensed larvae have a strong self-preservation instinct and will stimulate the mind of its host to the cause of excitement.

> *Such a well-fed larva can become fatal to a sensitive or emotional individual, and numerous mental disturbances such as persecution-mania and similar are the result of it. How many people are living under the erroneous supposal to be haunted and destroyed by black magicians, whereas they are, in fact, victims of their own fancies, or putting it correctly: victims of the larva they have been creating themselves.[28]*

The magician is to use the banishing pentagram of the earth at least twice a day and he is to use the soul mirror methods to ward off manifestations of fear, grief, sorrow, hatred and envy, and he is to have the servitor help him verify if any astral larvae remain. If none remains, he moves on to make a servitor of Sublimated Sex still with the earth element. That the servitor reveals visibly to the magician his own astral phantoms of eroticism is the objective. Franz Bardon[29] describes them as being born from the face or body of a person and provoking lust. The more the love and longing of the enamoured one is unsatisfied the more the yearning grows, increasing the insinuations of the phantom who thrives on thoughts of this nature. The phantom shows in dreams, awakening love first and later allowing sexual intercourse, becoming denser and increasingly influencing the host whose own willpower diminishes. The host becomes confused, stops eating, the nerves are over-excited and the phantom eventually starts to appear in hallucinations, possibly leading to the suicide of the victim of unsatisfied passion and of non-corresponded love.

---

[27] Franz Bardon, *Initiation into Hermetics* (Germany: Rüggeberg-Verlag, 1993), 132.

[28] Franz Bardon, *Initiation into Hermetics* (Germany: Rüggeberg-Verlag, 1993),132.

[29] Franz Bardon, *Initiation into Hermetics* (Germany: Rüggeberg-Verlag, 1993), 133.

If, after using the soul mirror and the banishing pentagram of the earth for some time, there is no phantom of eroticism left, the magician goes on to make the servitor of the sublimated fight-or-flight instinct, which is to be filled with the element of fire, with the proposal of having it uncover any possible fight-or-flight phantoms. The soul mirror is always to be put to use and, in this case, the banishing pentagram of the fire. Of phantasms, Bardon brings us the following description:

> *A larva is quite unconsciously adopting a shape in the mental sphere, appropriate to the motive of the single or repeated psychic emotion, whereas a phantom accepts a certain form originating in the fantasy of Man.[30]*

Bardon gives us the example of a mysterious man sighted by the host of this soon to be phantom. The host starts placing the blame of everyday incidents on the type of man, leading to a feeling of persecution. The image of the type of man becomes more distinct, who visits in dreams and eventually emerges in broad daylight. The host's involuntary lively imagination can condense this man to the point that it becomes visible to other persons. The phantom causes nervous breakdowns, insanity and suicide.

When there is no phantom left to be revealed, the time comes when the magician must create the servitor of sublimated clanning, to be filled with water, giving him the sole mission of showing the magician, visibly, any hidden phantasms on his mental or astral sphere. Here, together with the soul mirror, the banishing pentagram of the water is put to use regularly. Of phantasms, it was written:

> *Remembering, praising, mourning the deceased, any memory of or tribute to them will create and enliven imaginary pictures of the dead, which as a result of frequent repetition, have a rather long duration of life. We call these pictures, created by the living ones, phantoms. It is this kind of phantom that manifest themselves, in great numbers, to the so-called spiritualists, evokers, diviners, etc. The spooks and hobgoblins also are nothing else but phantoms preserving, condensing and thriving on the affection and*

---

[30] Franz Bardon, *Initiation into Hermetics* (Germany: Rüggeberg-Verlag, 1993), 133.

attachment of the bereaved ones, as it happens in the case of the shadows.[31]

When all that has been cleansed, there is no further need to climb up to the spectres of the other instincts, as the human being generally needs them in order to connect functionally to the remaining members of his species.

Taming of the Pegasus

It is time for the magician to build his own "alphabet of desire", an expression used first by Austin Osman Spare and then Peter Carroll. The magician is to get a good number of coins, paint them, and draw on them symbols referring to all the virtues that are in his personal soul mirror together with all the virtues of the soul mirrors we gave him. These coins are to be painted white. Faults, lack, and so on, are also to be represented in such a way, and the coins are to be covered in black paint first. Some coins are mandatory; either the magician has them on his soul mirror or not, such as the white coins of love, life, passion, power, death, wisdom, devotion and the black coins of anxiety, insecurity, vulnerability, doubt, delusion, stagnation.

General coins should be middle-sized, root virtues or defects should be large coins, and principles should be the largest coins, such as the forgotten ones, the sublimated instincts, the four hermetic principles, the akashic or cosmic virtues, and the letters. The less influence a virtue or a defect has, the smaller the coin. The symbols painted on the coins are to have the colour of the elements the virtues or faults are attributed to, but, in cases such as the akashic virtues, they are to be painted in violet. The symbols must represent, in the mind of the magician, the energies and intentions of the attribute.

Then the magician imposes his hands on all the coins relating to the white mirror and charges them with vital fluid, then with the element through the use of the corresponding invoking pentagram, and finally draws in the energy connected with the aspects of the sigils. The coins of the black mirror should be charged in such a way that the coins represent not an expression of the traits, as in the white mirror, but a prison blocking the vices from their very roots, and are to be charged with the banishing

---

[31] Franz Bardon, *Initiation into Hermetics* (Germany: Rüggeberg-Verlag, 1993), 136-137.

87

pentagrams that can, at any time, be reversed to allow the magician the use of the destructive forces. The black coins should, therefore, have a counter positive trait painted on the other side, in order to seal them and neutralise them, while the coins of the white mirror are to have a complementary virtue on their other side, in order to empower them.

It is sufficient for the magician to arrange different coins in any order that serves his desired effect, place them in front of him, and read it with the spirit looking through the astral and the physical senses in order to perform an adequate conjuration of the desired combinations or else an exorcism. In order to attain coherence on the astral, he can charge these different coins so that they, standing together, mix their auras into a single fluid, on which the magician is to create the elementary and send him on a mission according to his will. The magician can also simply meditate with each coin to gain further guidance, and he should, for it is his job to later learn how to write and think with these symbols. In order to do that, the magician is to learn divination through his own coins, not so that he learns how to read the future in the coins, but that he learns how to interpret any situation according to their language. It is important that the magician's divinations are to his mind but simulations; he is not to put faith into the casting of the coins, for if he did, he would be performing a random conjuration instead, the reason why many tarot readers end up causing much misfortune to their clients and to themselves.

He can start with a casting of three coins in a horizontal line, the left for the past, the one in the centre for the present time, and the one in the right for the future. Above the coin of the centre, he is to put one other coin, and the same is to be done below. The coin above represents the active or aggressive influence, the coin below represents the passive, blocked or inert influence over the cross hold of the present time. Let him try different combinations and finally just throw a handful of coins taken randomly and learn to figure out the meaning that is being presented to him. He can start reading from the centre and follow clockwise to simulate divining the future, or counterclockwise to read into the past.

To further deepen the magician's perceptions of his "alphabet of desire" he can fuse coins together as taught above when we explained to the magician how to fuse the aura of the coins together, creating a ball. He then is to transfer his consciousness to the depth point of the ball, meditate, come back to his body and imagine a cosmic ball around him exactly like the one he came from. He draws the powers of that specific cosmos into himself until he and the fused fluid become one, then he is to write as he did before through the akashic virtues. He should try nine combinations at least, with nine texts accordingly. Then he is still to translate the texts into the language of his alphabet of desire, which might seem difficult at first, but the magician's creativity and intuition should have become by now self-sufficient. We can give, nonetheless, an example. Let's say the magician has written the following: "'I saw the palace of the void standing on a silver stone". The word "I" may be translated as the symbol of the quality of ego-consciousness, the word "saw" can be translated to any coin representing capacities of observation, the word "the" as any capacity analogous to the power of consciousness transference, the word "palace", referring to a house of sorts, can be translated into any coin-related with awareness and consciousness, but because a palace is a house of greatness, any coin relating to greatness can be added. The void translates into coins related to the qualities of silence or to the virtue of connection to the supreme source. Standing relates to virtues of self-preservation, balance or stability. Silver may relate to the most noble attributes of water or to the quality of disclosing mystery, and stone, to the virtue of supreme dominion. When the magician is confused as to how to translate certain words, let him divide the conceptual elements present in those words and translate the key components, bringing them together in the phrase under construction. When expertise has been achieved, the magician will become a skilled decipherer in any symbolic system, and he may choose to start writing in his journal through the single-use of his "alphabet of desire". If certain attributes are missing for him to express himself freely, he is to enter akashic trance and search for them, so that his language and awareness evolves the more original qualities he finds.

Taming of the Horse

What we will prescribe to the magician here is not much different from what is given by Bardon at Step VII of *Initiation Into Hermetics*, but it is adapted to the aim and spirit of the present work.

The magician is to write down a soul mirror with the divisions being: will, intellect, emotions/feelings, consciousness. The will is to have the positive trait of "strong will" and the negative traits of "stubbornness" and "weakness". He examines himself and tries to fight stubbornness, if he has any, with the teachings and tools that have been given in this book. But he will fight "weakness" by reaching out to the eyes with his will and have it seeing through his eyes, transmuting fire into light. Let him often enjoy the colours, shades and distinguish the different layers in the spectres of natural light radiation. His volition will be magnetised by such exercises and he will witness his weak will decreasing and his strong will increasing.

The intellect is to have the positive traits of "high level of performance" and "maturity" and the negative trait called "weak intellect". He will ward off his weakness, if there is any, through reaching out to the ear with his intellect and have the intellect hearing through his ear, letting air transform into sound. Let him often enjoy, in this way, music, the natural sound of the landscape, silence, and so on. The sound should become a world in itself. The same effect will happen as it did before with fire and volition, the attributes of maturity and high performance intensifying by having been magnetised.

To eliminate emotional weakness and lack of feelings the magician will allow his feeling capacity to reach out to his perception, transforming water into emotions. Let him linger in this way, enjoying existence with no other preoccupation.

Now, under the division of "consciousness," there are the traits of slow thoughts and depression. If any manifest, the magician will dissipate them by allowing consciousness to touch the sense of taste and smell, transforming the earth element into the expansion of consciousness, letting himself become what he smells and what he tastes. This will alleviate the acuteness of his thoughts and depression will lose its burden.

As a sign of success that all these elements have been balanced and put to equal performance, the magician will see a rising feeling of realisation, and his consciousness will tend more and more towards his conscience, the essence of his own being.

Step 13

The magician will, at this time, pick from his "alphabet of desire" just the coins specific to the letters we had him working previously, they being:

Fire:

C
Active Quality: Self Spiritualisation
Passive Quality: Divine Ideas

D
Active Quality: Creativity
Passive Quality: Ego-consciousness in all elemental analogies

H
Active Quality: Power of the Word
Passive Quality: Understanding of Divine Providence

K
Active Quality: Standing pure and above all things
Passive Quality: Faith

S
Active Quality: Contact with the divine Spirit
Passive Quality: Prophecy

Sh
Active Quality: Highest enlightenment
Passive Quality: Spiritual-ecstasy

T
Active Quality: Divine inspiration
Passive Quality: Invention

Air:

A
Active Quality: Highest wisdom
Passive Quality: High intelligence

L
Active Quality: Virtue
Passive Quality: Morality

Z
Active Quality: Cognition
Passive Quality: Talent

Water:

G
Active Quality: Grace
Passive Quality: Peacefulness

Ch
Active Quality: Clarity
Passive Quality: Oratory skills

J
Active Quality: Love
Passive Quality: Ecstasy

M
Active Quality: Fluidity
Passive Quality: Clear feelings and acute sensations

N
Active Quality: Happiness
Passive Quality: Unison of emotion and intellect

W
Active Quality: Intuition
Passive Quality: Mediumistic faculties

Earth:

B
Active Quality: Cognition of polarity
Passive Quality: Influence over fate

F
Active Quality: Harmony
Passive Quality: Unification of faculties

I
Active Quality: Evolution
Passive Quality: Memory

O
Active Quality: Justice
Passive Quality: Judgement

P
Active Quality: Spiritualisation
Passive Quality: Devotion

R
Active Quality: Independence
Passive Quality: Maturity

Ae
Active Quality: Transformation
Passive Quality: Seeing through all thoughts, desires and wishes

Setting them aside, he will accumulate the element of light, compressing it into his eyes so as to achieve radiation. He is to remember that the element is shining, penetrating and expanding. He is to breathe it in with the quality of clairvoyance. While the eyes are radiating with rays of clairvoyant light he can direct them anywhere to see anything in time and space. He is also to remember that it is the spirit that is looking through his eyes. He will devise a topic and throw in the coins, and read them, his mind not being interpretative this time, but passive to the visual impressions of clairvoyance alone. This step makes the magician a true specialist of divination, where before he was only simulating and training his skills as a decipherer. At the end, the magician should disperse the light.

The same is to be repeated with clairaudience, making use of the air element and the ears. After such has been done, we can make use of what Bardon[32] prescribes: we should introduce the akashic principle into the head via imagination and transfer our consciousness into our ears. Imagination proceeds then to engage with the faculty of absolute clairaudience through the akasha principle that inhabits the ears and we resort to our astral sense of hearing.

The magician now throws the coins and reads them through hearing by clairaudience. As an alternative, he can charge one ear alone, and press the magical cup against it in order to hear the messages.

Next, he will try divination through clairsentience, also known as clairfeeling, about which Bardon writes in *Initiation Into Hermetics*[33].

The term clairsentience means the capacity to perceive and feel all occurring in the elements and in akasha. Some know it as psychometry, the power to read an object in either the past, present or the future. Some know it as the power to materialise thought and being, or as the skill of intuition. All such faculties are of the field of clairfeeling.

The magician is to accumulate the water element in his whole body and load it with the intense imagination of clairfeeling until he is absolutely sure of it. Then, he is to imagine that his entire body is swimming in the universal water element, as if in the centre of the surface of an endless ocean. He feels nothing but water, accumulating magnetism. This magnetism will enliven the finest particles of his sensation-fields and produce the astral clairfeeling. First, in the forehead, then in the heart, next

---

[32] Franz Bardon, *Initiation into Hermetics* (Germany: Rüggeberg-Verlag, 1993), 149.

[33] Franz Bardon, *Initiation into Hermetics* (Germany: Rüggeberg-Verlag, 1993), 150-152.

comes the solar plexus, and finally the hands and thighs. Then he turns his clairfeeling to the subject at hand, reading the coins that have been thrown.

When clairvoyance, clairaudience and clarifeeling have become natural, the magician will have no trouble using the three simultaneously, loading them in sequence and then, after his work is done, dissipating the accumulations.

Taming of the Pegasus

In this exercise, we will be making use of a crystal ball. Preparing and operating the crystal ball has been taught in-depth in my book *The Path of IPSOS*[34] and I may quote the essentials directly from there:

The magician is to choose a crystal sphere that calls him in to be as perfect as it itself is. He takes the crystal between his hands, turns his eyes inward and upward and thinks of the highest ideals only. When all is holy, the magician looks upon the crystaline, its lucid depth, and receives ideas of purity back, allowing him to become a child. On the crystal globe, he will perceive the astral light of the globe absorbing every single emanation, vibrating it and absorbing it anew into the senses and into consciousness. Then the magician will unite index and thumb in a circle and condensate there the astral light with the quality of the highest ideal. An electromagnetic membrane will appear to him similar to a bubble of light between his hands. He is to pass it through the crystalline globe, filtering the influences of the astral light that go through the crystal. He then repeats, but his index fingers and thumbs forming a triangle, he thinks of the highest ideal on its purest form on the mental, astral and physical sense, and again has the triangle pass through the crystal, this time touching it afterwards with his hands and rubbing it until it becomes warm. The thoughts of the magician are to be kept on the highest ideal, which the magician gives, as something that is the core of his own life, to the crystal ball.

----

[34] Andre Consciencia, *The Path of IPSOS* (Sirius Lmited Esoterica, 2020).

We will use the enlivened crystal ball in order to communicate with our holy guardian angel or spiritual guide, about which Franz Bardon[35], writes, stating that it is assigned by Divine Providence at the hour of birth, being a deceased person or an intellectual entity not embodied on this planet that protects, guides and inspires the scholar of magic.

The first thing the magician is to practise is clairvoyance, making use of the crystal ball as a medium in order to obtain his spiritual guide's sigil. Next, he will ask him for his appearance.

Later, the magician will make use of clairaudience and ask of the being for the best times to contact him. Then he will ask him about his soul mirror, making notes, and later comparing his own soul mirror with that of his guide, and writing down a soul mirror with the faculties of his spiritual guide that he lacks, working on them with the keys that have been given to him by us, and through clairfeeling, using the ball to sense these faculties directly from his guide and breathing them in into himself.

To meet his guide on this plane, the magician can create astral densification with his appearance, charging it with fire on the head, air on the chest, water on the abdominal region, and earth at the limbs and waist. Then he fills it inwardly with the different akashic virtues that he has come to learn and, making use of clairvoyance, clairaudience and clairfeeling, calls the being from the crystal into his homunculi. When the conversation is over, he is to help his guide go back to the akasha through the crystal ball and to dissolve the shape that he has prepared for him to inhabit.

Taming of the Horse

We leave the magician to perfect his training of Qi Kung, Tai Chi, Shaolin Kung Fu, Yoga, stick Tai Chi and Sword Tai Chi without further burdening him. But, if it is his will, let him learn Dervish Dancing.

---

[35] Franz Bardon, *Initiation into Hermetics* (Germany: Rüggeberg-Verlag, 1993), 118.

$\mathcal{S}$tep 14

It is now suitable for the magician to create his elementaries, who are able to operate down to the physical plane if it is of the magician's choice.

As a first exercise, the magician will dedicate himself to the crystal ball. He will fill it, by accumulating in his own body and then radiating, with clairvoyance, clairaudience and clairfeeling, so that the ball has the mission to transmit to him immediately all that it captures according to the magician's commands. The elementary will look like a radiating sun surrounded by wind and sea, its rays of light reaching beyond that atmosphere in different colours. The ball must be given a name and its lifetime should be set, also the magician must determine how the elementary is to be destroyed by him when such a need arrives. Then the magician orders it to hide in the crystal ball until further notice.

About the destruction of the elementary, Bardon has written:

If the time you had fixed beforehand has expired, make certain with the help of the pendulum that the elementary has returned into its form. If so, you can then dissolve the elementary in the way you previously determined, namely by burning its name, with the help of a special ritual, or by spelling its name backwards in an undertone.[36]

Gaming of the Pegasus

The magician is now to go back to the sublimated instincts and form an elementary for each one of them, but an elementary requires greater effort. A figurine for each one is required, which the magician will place on a form of sanctuary, for they are to serve him as the saints of the believer, being, in a way, his devas. For this we will mostly and modestly quote from Bardon[37], as our method for the construction of these figures and the way to bring them to life is like his, with only some minor and slight changes.

---

[36] Franz Bardon, *Initiation into Hermetics* (Germany: Rüggeberg-Verlag, 1993), 157-158.

[37] Franz Bardon, *Initiation into Hermetics* (Germany: Rüggeberg-Verlag, 1993), 159.

Take two parts by volume of loam and one part of wax. Stir the loam with some warm water to a thick pulp and add the beeswax, either completely melted or warmed to softness. Knead both ingredients until they are very well mixed.

The magician then forms the figure according to the image he has of the sublimated instinct. He gives it the desired shape and with a pointed object sinks an opening while the doll is still warm. A large hollow inside the figure should be produced from head to feet, following down the spine, and the hollow filled with fluid condenser. The opening is to be closed while the figure is soft or, if it has cooled down and hardened, it should be sealed with liquid wax.

In our case, the fluid condenser is blood and semen or seminal fluid. The wax figure is held with the left hand and rubbed with the right hand in order to be animated with vital power. A blow of breath is to give life to the figure and the developing elementary is to receive a name, spoken several times into it.

Now, the magician fills his whole body with a certain element and, through it, he fills the corresponding part of the body of the figure with the same element. Because the sublimated ones have been given to specific elements from the beginning, we will use four different grades of each element. For instance, if the sublimated one is connected with the earth element, the magician will fill his whole body with solid steel earth and project it outward to the limbs and waist of the figure. A state of the earth element more similar to stone is accumulated and projected to the abdominal region of the figurine. The state of clay is projected to the chest and pure crystal to the head. The materials symbolise different states of the dynamic density of the element. But in any case, the magician will then impregnate the fluids with gravity with the firm conviction that the earth element will remain in the figure and work constantly.

Sublimated instincts related to water, limbs and waste are to be charged with the density of ice, the abdominal region with the density of resins or oils, the chest with water, and the head with vapour.

Sublimated instincts related to air, limbs and waste are to be charged with the compact density of the vacuum, the abdominal region with the density of whirlwinds, the chest with flowing winds, and the head with the still air.

99

Sublimated instincts related to fire, limbs and waste are to be charged with the density of coal, the abdominal region with the density of lava, the chest with fire, and the head with light.

Then Bardon[38] writes that as soon as the four elements have been projected into the figure the astral body of the elementary is ready and has adopted the doll's shape. The elementary can be emanated from the doll and adopt any prefered size. From there on the elementary is connected to the doll and depends on it to exist, being bound to reassume the size of the doll and re-enter it after the accomplished task. Imagination produces in the doll the mental body made from etheric matter, and this mental body surrounds and wraps the form of the physical doll. The properties of mind and soul which the elementary is to possess are to be concentrated and deepened in the doll's head by meditation.

In this case, we will want to give the sublimated instinct all the subordinated virtues, strengths and qualities that are under that instinct in our soul mirror, excluding the four divine principles, the virtues corresponding to cosmic letters and others that we have given the magician during the course of this book.

Franz Bardon[39] continues, telling us to accumulate in our right hand light from the universe, so that the right hand becomes shiny, fiery and hot like the sun. The left hand holds the figure and the right hand is placed above it. A warm breath should be offered to the navel region of the doll and the name of the elementary spoken into it while the light of the right hand moves to the puppet. During the first blow of breath, the magician imagines the heart of the doll starts to beat, the blood circulation and life becoming distinctly felt. On the seventh blow of breath, the light of the right hand finishes its migration into the doll and the astral form of the elementary throbs with life. On the eighth exhalation should have the astral body of the figure beginning to breathe autonomously. On the ninth exhalation, the name of the elementary is shouted aloud and a verbal command is given for it to live, in the form of an enthusiastic exclamation, vibrant with unshakable faith that a perfect being has been brought into the world.

---

38 Franz Bardon, *Initiation into Hermetics* (Germany: Rüggeberg-Verlag, 1993), 161.

39 Franz Bardon, *Initiation into Hermetics* (Germany: Rüggeberg-Verlag, 1993), 162.

The magician, traditionally, then wraps the figure in silk, insulating it, and hides it from sight. In our case, we will want to have our sanctuary hidden from sight and enclosed by a silk curtain. The figures, inside, should also be wrapped in silk, to be unwrapped whenever used. Unwrapping them should immediately project them. Also, unless the magician wishes to destroy the being, he must not wrap the figure while the elementary is released, for it will kill the elementary. Never forget that the purpose and task of the elementary is to be incorporated into it as it is created.

In our case, we shall give the elementary the mission of charging the magician's virtues corresponding with the sublimated instinct and to weaken opposite faults and vices whenever preyed upon. A ritual to confine the elementary to its body or to release it should also be assigned from the start, and it should be sufficient to trace the banishing pentagram of the element corresponding to the figure while saying its name, in order to confine it.

The magician is not to destroy the figure abruptly before dissolving or absorbing its attributes and fluids, for it will cause him damage through sympathetic magic. To solve such problems, Bardon instructs us to prepare a bath as hot as can be endured and get in with the figurine wrapped in silk and held in the left hand. While the left hand shakes off the silk, the right hand, being loaded with akasha, directs its beam of destruction to the figure's heart. While this is being done, the doll is dipped below the water and its whole vitality and being passes through the water to our own vitality and being. Whatever is not tolerable remains in the water until it cools down and is drained off together with the fluid condenser. What remains of the doll is at this stage burnt or buried together with the silk.

Magicians can also create figurines out of the instincts in their raw states and feed them elementaries which they are then able to connect to the global instinct of the species itself, influencing whole villages, cities, countries or the world at large. But this is not our work at *Through the Soul Mirror.*

Next, the magician is going to grab a flat square of metal and draw two squares intertwined. At each square, he will draw, at the corners, a triangle for the fire, a circle for the air, a crescent for the water and a cube for the earth. At one square he draws a plus at the symbols and at the other a minus. Inside he is to place the sword and accumulate or radiate so much fire in or at the surface of the metal that it creates a spark. He continues

101

until it becomes like a flame of a candle, and will strive to make it grow wider. Finally, he has the flame take on the shape of the sword, through imagination, fuses the fire with the sword, and impregnates it with absolute victory, thereby creating the elementary under the prescriptions that have been taught. The mission of this elementary should be to bring absolute victory to the one holding the sword.

The same is to be repeated with the staff, the element being that of air, the elementary should bestow supreme wisdom to the beholder of the staff. With the cup, the water should be compressed until it reaches the size of an ice cube and further, and the elementary is to immediately uncover any secret to the owner of the cup. The elementary of the pentacle is to be done with the earth element, it compressing until forming a diamond and so on, gifting the master of the pentacle with the blessing of being supremely connected with the divine source. The lamp is to be worked with the element of light, compressed until forming a sun, the work of the elementary being to connect the magician with his inner light at all times. The hat is to be loaded with the akasha, compressed until forming a black egg radiating violet light, and so is the robe and the belt. Upon request, the elementary of the hat has the mission to reveal the perfection of anything and anyone, including the magician; the elementary of the robe has the mission to insulate the magician; the elementary of the belt has the mission to connect any individual aspects of the magician with the corresponding cosmic actions.

Finally, the coins of the cosmic letters are to undergo the magical animation of graphics. The magician is to recharge each coin once again with their corresponding element, colour and virtue and, needing no fluid condenser as the metal and the paint should suffice, transfers his imagination of a mental body into the coin and then transfers the properties of the spirit: will, intellect, feeling and consciousness. They should stand radiating from inside the mental body, and the magician is to cover that mental body again with the letter, its virtue being its inspiration and its element being the sphere of action: this is the astral body of the elementary. The remaining procedures have been known to the magician. Finally, such elementaries can go beyond the capacities of the letters if they are pushed so far and should be given missions such as:

Fire:

C
Colour: Vermillion
Active Quality: Self-spiritualisation-
Passive Quality: Divine ideas
Mission: To change the qualities of a certain object

D
Colour: Dark blue
Active Quality: Creativity
Passive Quality: Ego-consciousness in all elemental analogies
Mission: To cause fertility or aid in procreation

H
Colour: Silver violet
Active Quality: Power of the word
Passive Quality: Understanding of Divine Providence
Mission: To learn and teach the Qabbalah

K
Colour: Silver blue
Active Quality: Standing pure and above all things
Passive Quality: Faith
Mission: To bring terrestrial treasures

S
Colour: Purple
Active Quality: Contact with the divine Spirit
Passive Quality: Prophecy
Mission: To learn of consciousness and its complete control, transmitting it to the magician

Sh
Colour: Red
Active Quality: Highest enlightenment
Passive Quality: Spiritual ecstasy

Mission: To learn and teach about the fire element in the mineral, vegetable and animal kingdoms

T
Colour: Dark brown
Active Quality: Divine inspiration
Passive Quality: Invention
Mission: To discover and teach the analogies of all kingdoms

Air:

A
Colour: Light blue
Active Quality: Highest wisdom
Passive Quality: High intelligence
Mission: To learn and teach the air element

L
Colour: Dark Green
Active Quality: Virtue
Passive Quality: Morality
Mission: To make the magician healthier and more beautiful

Z
 Colour: Lemon yellow
Active Quality: Cognition
Passive Quality: Talent
Mission: To entertain

Water:

G
Colour: Grass green
Active Quality: Grace
Passive Quality: Peacefulness
Mission: To bring about abundance

Ch
Colour: Violet
Active Quality: Clarity
Passive Quality: Oratory skills
Mission: To learn and teach about the water element

J
Colour: Dark opal
Active Quality: Love
Passive Quality: Ecstasy
Mission: To learn and teach about sex

M
Colour: Blue-green
Active Quality: Fluidity
Passive Quality: Clear feelings and acute sensations
Mission: To cause attraction between two people

N
Colour: Flesh red
Active Quality: Happiness
Passive Quality: Unison of emotion and intellect
Mission: To learn and teach how to be a master over all animals

W
Colour: Lilac
Active Quality: Intuition
Passive Quality: Mediumistic faculties
Mission: To learn and teach truths, to uncover lies and deceptions

Earth:

B
Colour: Violet
Active Quality: Cognition of polarity
Passive Quality: Influence over fate
Mission: To cure diseases

F
Colour: Light green
Active Quality: Harmony
Passive Quality: Unification of faculties
Mission: To learn and teach the relation between physics and metaphysics

I

Colour: Opal
Active Quality: Evolution
Passive Quality: Memory
Mission: To learn and teach biology

O
Colour: Aquamarine
Active Quality: Justice
Passive Quality: Judgement
Mission: To bring about success and happiness

P
Colour: Grey
Active Quality: Spiritualisation
Passive Quality: Devotion
Mission: To learn and teach about parenthood

R
Colour: Gold
Active Quality: Independence

Passive Quality: Maturity
Mission: To learn and teach psychology

Ae
Colour: Light brown
Active Quality: Transformation
Passive Quality: Seeing through all thoughts, desires and wishes
Mission: To learn and teach hermetics

This is just an example, and the magician may easily find other suitable missions. Also, the magician can create an elementary to help someone else, and he must not, for this effect, have the elements pass through his body at the moment when he is loading the coins. He can choose to keep the coin, or give it to the one under his protection.

Step 15

Before we proceed we must do some more work on the soul mirror. The magician must check if there is any misplacement of his ego or a domineering intellect. Signs that he may be afflicted by such things may manifest as a conviction that the magician has attained to perfection whatever might be the case, or the strength of his emotions making him act against his ethics, being uncontrolled. He must also check for signs of submission to any other person. So, there is the square of "misplaced ego", the square of "domineering intellect", and the square of "cult of personality". Blasphemy is the result of a domineering intellect and degradation is the result of paying cult to personality, whether it is the magician's personality or another's personality. At this, he should also check if he has become attached to the devotion anyone is sending towards him. In the white mirror, there should be "respect" and "truth" and "reverence for the essential holiness" as roots. Hope comes from respect. Faith comes from truth. Intelligence comes from a reverence for essential holiness.

Once this is out of the way we are to explore mental projection or the so-called mental travelling. Explored in Bardon's *IIH,* is a method of training in which the magician becomes exactly as he is on the physical and learns to fix this form. Because our aim in *Through the Soul Mirror* is mostly in exploring introspection, we think this form could be limiting and so we will quote directly from our other book, *The Way of Abrahadabra* for the methodology. But the reader is encouraged to explore Bardon's methods simultaneously so that no part of his development is left unsolved. Be that as it may, we have to start exactly with Bardon's[40] method of preparation. That is, we must adopt our asana in front of the mirror, contemplate our reflected image and close our eyes, imagining our reflection with the mind. When the image in our mind is perfectly intact, and particular attention is given to the facial expression, we transplant our consciousness and embody it.

At this point we stand observing our body via the reflected image, impressing with our imagination every object near to it, until it becomes as natural as watching with the physical eyes.

---

[40] Franz Bardon, *Initiation into Hermetics* (Germany: Rüggeberg-Verlag, 1993), 176.

We also must imagine that it is our spirit that is perceiving everything and making use of the senses, moving around absolutely free from time and space but with the same distinction as if still connected with the physical body.

Now, we follow to *The Way of Abrahadabra*[41]:

The magician will lie down, relax, and flex his muscles, one by one. Each time he flexes a muscle and then relaxes it he shall maintain in his imagination the sensation of when the muscle was flexed and tense. When he has worked through the whole body, the magician will let the muscles that are being imagined rise above, leaving his own lying body behind. But let him move not forward, for the magician should refrain from walking with his mental body as he would with his physical body. His work is to make the mental body move by willpower alone. And at first let him explore freely until he is well versed in this art. When the magician is done he should just slip inside his physical body again and stretch, joining his mental body with his muscles once more. Proof of a successful mental projection is shown when the magician starts to see 360° around him.

After a while, it continues:

He will explore freely, but at the mental plane, he should by necessity meet the zones of memory, reason, intuition and cognition. At the mental dimension of memory, he should be able to find his memories. He will realize that they are not paralyzed, they live and they change and communicate. At the mental zone of reason he will understand the secrets of geometry and the architecture of all meaning. At the mental zone of intuition, he will understand time, again not as something chronological and stabilized, but something that flows in from the future to permeate the present and the past. At the mental zone of cognition, he will find raw ideas, ideas that are even before taking shape and direction, and shapes that are even before any idea is able to attach itself to it.

---

[41] Andre Consciencia, *The Way of Abrahadabra* (Sirius Limited Esoterica, 2019).

About this, we should keep in mind and action, using our magical diary and acting upon it, that sight comes from the removal of the veils of illusion, and this is the magician's work of refinement during his explorations of the mental plane. Also, he is to keep conscious that at the mental plane all that is lives and all that lives is intelligent.

In another step, we add:

> *Now the magician should bring to mind a place from his childhood that he felt to be haunting and such place should have a hole, a passageway or an entrance, no matter how tiny. Let him take his mental body, explore that place and, with the firm intention of meeting his intellectual vices, go down that gate. He should find a tunnel or a corridor and go out on the first exit. Let him look around with the firm intention, again, of meeting his intellectual vices and persevere until one makes himself visible and available. The magician is to fix his attention on it and speak not; in time the mental personification of this vice will be forced by way of the magician's silence to speak and reveal itself. The job is to listen and not to talk. These sessions should occur until the magician knows that vice perfectly well by applying the methods of active listening. Next, he is to fix his will on the essence of this vice, focusing on the centre of the mental being representing it and he should not let go. When the magician can do this for ten minutes he will shift his awareness to the emptiness inside the personified vice. Ten minutes without further distractions should suffice. The magician will now inflict upon this void his own will, forcing the vice to swear to be obedient to the magician and never to harm him, and also commanding him to take an animal shape, for a vice can be restituted to its purity by bestiality, but also an animal may be taught to obey a man.*
>
> *He should find and bind at least four mental vices, as abstract as they may appear at the beginning: one for cognition, one for memory, one for reason and one for intuition.*

Further indications are:

These spirits shall now be at his service and aid him whenever called during the magician's projections, never working against his conscious will no matter if he is at his mental and astral travels or down on earth. The magician is to gather from them, once they have been turned to beasts, their names and powers. At each of these regions, the magician shall also find a virtuous master, but these masters have to be tested, for when the magician finds their emptiness, that emptiness shall be so light-hearted that the magician has no way in which to manipulate it and shape it except by becoming one with it and to learn. While his now transmuted vices are meant to protect the magician aggressively, the masters are meant to guide him passively. For practical reasons and later developments, the magician should also ask of such beings, negative or positive, their energetic signatures: a reunion of symbols, curves and shapes that remain as a mental or an astral translation of their inner structures...

Now, as a fine method to find these masters the magician shall ride his corresponding vices, that is, let him mount the vice of his instincts to find his guide on that same subject, and ride him through a mountain up to the pole star. There, let him find initiation and further guidance. When the magician is entering the underworld or the upper world he should focus on the particular aspect of the plane he is to explore, that is, "at the first door to the underworld I find the region of memory in the mental plane and the personification of my vice therein". At the upper world, while the magician is making use of the Ursa Major, he will notice that each of the seven stars harbours a door.

Later, we add:

The magical diary of the magician could be prepared as follows regarding the mentioned journeys:

Vice:
Region:

Name:
Sigil:
Shell:
Shadow:
Animal:
The magick of the animal:

The magician envisions the shell when he first sights the vice or its personification, but it shifts when he concentrates on its essence and that is the shadow. Finally, when the magician can penetrate the vice's emptiness and subdue it from inside, it regains its purity through the shape of an animal and reveals its powers to aid the magician in his Great Work.

In some cases where the vice has become a personality trait and not just a state of mind or soul the shell and the shadow may be as one.

For virtues the magical diary should be filled as follows:

Virtue:
Region:
Name:
Sigil:
Outer shape:
Inner shape:

In such a case the virtue and its powers are as one, the outer shape is first sighted and when the magician focuses on the essence of the personification he finds the inner shape, while at its emptiness the magician finds his consciousness transmuted.

Our indications in *The Way of Abrahadabra* should be sufficient for now.

Taming of the Pegasus

Taking the above in consideration, we are to work further on the soul mirror and then advance to methods of astral projection. The magician is to check if he has a conscious awareness of unity between all his knowledge and his experience, and where this is not the case, we have detected an imbalance, for action and ethics will not be in accordance, and from it will arise self-destructing behaviours.

The magician, having advanced to the point where he is, is to keep his responsibility at all times, for he is a living talisman of humanity, and the species depends on his strife for personal perfection and, at the same time, he should check his soul mirror for any signs that he may be thinking of himself with such self-regard that he considers himself to be a saviour or messiah of sorts, and his sanity will depend on ever analysing his proper function in the world and also on him having the best possible enlightened self-interest, for anything else might come as a mutilation to the structures of the ego-consciousness, essential for the wholeness of the magician as an expression of awareness.

Whenever the magician thinks of redemption or salvation, he is to think instead of realisation and evolution, for redemption and salvation lag in the past and are corrosive aspects of the water emanating from melancholy.

The magician is to check his soul mirror for any signs of not being able to recognise another's spiritual maturity, or even communicating with another in a language that is not suitable to the spiritual maturity of his kindred. He is to communicate if sincerely asked to, in a way that is familiar, comfortable and compatible, the only exception being when he can bypass the verbal sensors of another's consciousness by works of art or by showing instead of preaching or by any other methods that succeed.

If the magician ever sees himself debating, arguing, proving or convincing with an attitude of trying to sell his spiritual ideas, he is to know that he is not working from a place of balance, for his stories should be for those interested in listening to them and no more. The magician is to keep in check, too, if his meddlings with magic are somehow keeping him from the true works of introspection and transformation, for this is the case of a paralysing presence of the willpower and one of the greatest dangers to any magician. On the soul mirror, he is to put excessive self-importance against the capacity for wonderment, and it will become clear to him what is in his enlightened self-interest. Under the fault of excessive self-importance are subordinate vices such as assuming sanctity and taking credit for ecstasy. But faults may also arise from the virtue of wonderment, such as the magician being left unearthed and not putting inspiration into practice.

At last, the magician will set his timer strategically to four times a day, so that when it goes off the magician puts special attention to his breath, imagining that it is the spirit that is breathing through the body with the mediation of the astral body. When this has become second nature, he is to perform as quoted from our book, *The Way of Abrahadabra*[42], not forgetting to breathe once in the astral body:

> *Afterwards, using his mental body, let him concentrate at the centre of his physical body, sucking all the emotional density out of it into his mental bolt. Then let him journey. Proof of success is that the magician will now be able to listen to actual whispers, he will be more empathic with his surroundings and his senses on the astral will deepen. When such journeys have become natural and the magician does them without effort, he should, now using the combination of his mental and astral bodies, concentrate on the dot at the centre of his physical body and, by willpower, suck the nervous strain there into himself, so that his senses and the instruments of his sensibility will become very similar to the ones at the physical plane, and he should be able to interact with the events of the physical world either in the past, the present or the future.*

We continue to quote:

> *In the astral, he should at least explore the zone of feelings, emotions, sensations and that zone of pure light. Feelings are energies that were given some meaning and significance while emotions are just energies in motion, they move and live with a life devoid of the need for meaning. Sensations are mostly of the etheric plane, they are meant to be energy attached to the physical senses and moulded by them. The*

---

[42] Andre Consciencia, *The Way of Abrahadabra* (Sirius Limited Esoterica, 2019).

zone of pure light is where all astral forms are but variations of pure vibration, they are trespassed by the light of their own astral source in such a way that they are rendered invisible.

And:

He should find and bind at least four astral vices, appertaining to the so-called soul mirror: one for his instincts, one for his own light oscillation, one for his sense of meaning and one for his emotions. For the astral realm, the door in which the magician should turn when on his tunnel is the second, except when dealing with the instincts, it being the third.

For the remaining part, the procedure is the same as when we dealt with our vices through mental wandering. But, about the counter-virtues, it is added:

When the magician is to ride his animals up to the masters of his virtues he should leave either on the mental, astral or etheric plane and call forward the name of the animal as a vibration and visualise the sigil emanating on the air and shifting reality like a magnet of dreams. The animal is to appear. Each star of the Ursa Major is a door to a master, but the door to the astral region of light is the constellation Ursa Major itself, as a whole.

It should be common knowledge that, at the end of his adventures, the magician is to return properly to his physical body, giving it all the mental, astral and etheric vitality back by penetrating it and breathing through it. There is a magnet attracting the magician's astral body to his physical body: the magician has but to give in so to be pushed back.

ซtep 16

The magician is to try the inductive method taught by Bardon in IIH on the subject of controlling the electric fluid. He does the accumulation of fire as taught. Bardon explains again in here the method, without giving much importance to the inhalations and exhalations, given that the magician just keeps breathing naturally while swallowing the fire with his whole body.

This red fire is to be hot and bright like the sun. Warmth in the periphery of the body is automatically felt as well as an inner expansion of the fire element as the universal fire presses into the hollow body. The universal fire ball is to be imagined as intense and fiery as light presses through the pores of the skin and the body shines swollen with light. This pressure comes from the outside to the inside until we recognize the sensation that we are ready to burst.

Then an indication is given to the magician that tells him not to hold his breath, and Bardon[43] continues:

> *As soon as you have produced so strong an accumulation of light, namely a light-dynamide, that your body is bursting, you will feel at the same moment that your whole body, mainly your fingertips, has been loaded with a strong electric current. Impress this perception very firmly on your mind, because this is actually the electric fluid I am talking about.*

and later he goes on, to explain how to perform a desire impregnation on the electric fluid:

> *All you have to do is imagine that the light accumulated inside you, or better to say, the electric fluid contained in the light, reinforces and increases your active powers in the spirit, soul and body. In this manner, you can arouse all the active faculties, qualities, etc. that are imputed to the fire element and the air element in yourself.*

---

[43] Franz Bardon, *Initiation into Hermetics* (Germany: Rüggeberg-Verlag, 1993), 185.

Our aim is for the magician to perform the exercise and, when he is in the trance of the electric fluid, have him meditate on the enlargement and empowerment of his active faculties for fifteen to thirty minutes a day during a week. The magician's active qualities are easy to spot, they are in his soul mirror book. But this exercise must be, each day, immediately followed by the one we are about to give at the Taming of the Pegasus section.

Taming of the Pegasus

The method is similar, but the magician will be working with water and magnetism. About this, Bardon[44] writes:

> *Now close your eyes and imagine the whole universe being filled with water and yourself in the centre of it. You will automatically perceive the wetness and coolness on the periphery of your body, but do not give your full attention to this fact, imagine how your body similar to a dry sponge, thrown into the water, is sucking in the magnetic power from the universal water element. This imagination exercise must be permanently increased, until you feel a "dynamide" in yourself, similar to a fully inflated pneumatic tire, and until you are quite certain that a higher accumulation is impossible.*

later adding that by discriminating the difference between the electric and magnetic fluids we are rendered able to strenghten in ourselves the qualities dwelling in the water and earth elements.

In order to achieve our objectives at *Through the Soul Mirror*, the magician is to perform this exercise while still empowered by the electric fluid and his active faculties, so that they, in turn, excite the passive faculties and qualities, which the magician is to have close to him in his soul mirror books.

When this is done the magician compresses both fluids in different regions of the body as was suggested by Bardon[45] , and dynamically loads

---

[44] Franz Bardon, *Initiation into Hermetics* (Germany: Rüggeberg-Verlag, 1993), 186.

[45] Franz Bardon, *Initiation into Hermetics* (Germany: Rüggeberg-Verlag, 1993), 189.

the feet up to the pit of the stomach with magnetic fluid, and the head down to the chest with electric fluid. This he must do until getting the sensation that he is about to burst. Retaining both fluids, the magician presses with the help of imagination the electric fluid into the right beast, forming a hollow around the heart region. The magnetic fluid is moved and compressed to the left breast and from it to the left hand, that fills with cooling radiation. The electric fluid, in turn, must move from the right breast to the right hand, this hand becoming expansive, hot and electric.

With the hands loaded in this way, he will follow down to the Taming of the Horse.

Taming of the Horse

Having his right hand fully charged with the electric fluid and radiating, and his left hand with the magnetic fluid accordingly, the magician will now use his hands to heal his body. Both hands are to be laid on parts of the body simultaneously, and while the magician is passing to the next sequence, he must never disconnect both hands from the body at the same time, so that one hand changes position and only then the other is moved. While the hands are in the different regions of the body, they are to transmit the electric and magnetic fluids with the intention of fully restoring the functions and tissues of the body.

He starts by placing the right hand at the forepart and the left hand at the back of the head. He changes the left hand to the right side of the head and the right hand to the left.

He changes the right hand to the left ear and the left hand to the right ear, careful not to let the fluids go inside the ear hole.

The left hand changes to the right side of the neck, the right hand to the left side of the neck.

Both hands change to the forepart of the chest, one at a time, then the right hand goes to the forepart of the abdomen and the left hand to the back part. The right hand changes to the left side of the abdomen and the left hand to the right side.

He changes to one foot, the right hand at the left side of the foot and the left hand at the right side, and then he does exactly the same to the other foot.

If the magician is a male he changes both hands, one at the time, to the genitals, so that the right hand heals the forepart and the left hand the inside. If the magician is a female her left hand heals the forepart and her right hand the inside.

He changes the left hand to the region of the anus where the last vertebra stands. When this is done he releases the right hand, making sure it is finally unloaded, and, when he is ready, he releases the left hand at last.

This exercise must be repeated for 21 days. After 21 days, the body should reset to perfect harmony and become a natural conductor of electromagnetism.

tep 17

We will dedicate this step to the operation we call the alchemical exorcism. Some astral larvae, either they have grown to phantoms, phantasms, succubi, incubi, ghouls or vampires may have hidden from the magician when he was less mature. He will search for them, if there are any, with his clairvoyant, clairsentient and clairaudient abilities, or through mental and astral projection. Some may come from previous lifetimes, or other smaller astral larvae may have had the ability to respawn since last the magician checked.

For this effect, the magician will prepare a water recipient capable of taking heat, a cup, a piece of paper, and an apple. He will also prepare a fire. On the paper he writes the magical wish that any astral larvae, known or unknown, and under any form or state of maturity will most certainly and immediately be carbonised when feeding on and from the magician's fire. He charges the paper accordingly. The water in the cup is to be impregnated in such a way that whenever any astral larvae, known or unknown, and under any form or state of maturity when feeding on and from the magician's water will most certainly and immediately be poisoned. The water which is to take the heat will be impregnated likewise but concerning the magician's air element.

The magician ignites the fire under the water recipient, and in that fire he burns the paper, activating his spell. After a while, he drinks the water from the cup. He waits and when the water in the water recipient starts to vaporise, he activates the spell of air. When there is no drop left and all has been vaporised the magician lets the fire die.

He impregnates the apple with the wish that any larval seed of respawn left in connection with his consciousness be decomposed and utterly destroyed together with the pulp of the apple, and he inscribes this wish with any cutting object on the surface of the apple. Then he is to bury it deep below the place where the fire was ignited, letting the apple rot.

At any stage some apparitions may or may not take place, and it is best if the magician and his tools are protected by the magical circle. Nothing opposing the magician can enter the circle, and whatever happens outside the circle is not subject to the magician's attention.

Taming of the Pegasus

Fire:

The magician should take a glass frame where he is to frame a piece of aluminium paper or golden aluminium foil paper, depending on the use he is to give to his magical mirror. The paper, either the silver or the golden, should be wet with a liquid mixture, in equal parts, of angelica, sage, lime-tree flowers, cucumber skin, melon seed, acacia blossoms or leaves, chamomile flowers, lily flowers, leaves or roots, cinnamon flowers or bark, leaves of nettle, leaves of mentha peppermint, poplar leaves, leaves or flowers of sweet violet, osier leaves or bark, green or dry tobacco. For the first operation the golden aluminium foil paper is to be utilised.

The magician is to take onion, garlic, pepper, and mustard seed. He is to boil them with water, semen or the blood of the moon, and olive oil, the olive oil being impregnated with the virtues of responsibility, glory and authority. When it has become as a soup, the magician seals it in a recipient. During the course of 28 days he should sprinkle his magical weapons, ornaments, tools, coins and figurines related with the powers or virtues of the fire with the substance. Before the fluid condenser can be used the magician must make the liquid cold with ice, and before the magician is to sprinkle his magical objects, he must anoint the surface of the magical mirror with the same fluid condenser, so that when he is anointing the objects he imagines what they stand for becoming denser and also connecting with the mirror.

After 28 days have come to pass, he is to sit in front of the mirror, anoint the glass, and charge the mirror with the magical wish of it disintegrating immediately all astral larvae and have him connect with all his active and passive qualities of the fire together with his own elementals and elementaries connected with the fire element. He charges the mirror in such a way that it radiates through the whole room. He might do it with the help of the element fire and of the electric fluid. To the element air he uses the fluid of the air and the electric fluid. To water and earth he uses the elements and magnetism, the silver aluminium paper is to replace the golden aluminium.

Then he can act in a passive or active way.

121

The Passive Way:

The magician activates as taught his capacities of clairvoyance, clairfeeling and clairaudience, so that his threefold radiation is penetrating through the mirror just as the radiation of the mirror is penetrating through him. He calls in one of his virtues, strengths, powers, mights and so on to appear in the mirror. He can lay the object that has been attributed to it in front of the mirror if it makes it easier, or imagine the symbols of the coins in the surface of the mirror, but at the end he should be able to pass from virtue to virtue automatically without the aid of the objects. He asks the virtue, in whatever shape it may appear, whatever he wishes to learn and how else is it possible for the magician to cooperate with this virtue. He asks his virtues what are their faculties, how do they live, what are they in contact with and, overall, treats them as devas, living beings capable of miracles and with a life of their own. He may ask what are their true forms, powers and fluids, what planes do they have access to, how best can the virtue be impregnated, what are the virtue's best tools of influence, how do they like to communicate or receive input, he can ask them to prevent dangerous and undesirable influences, he can ask of them stories, and also their past, present and future, knowing that they are a part of him but communicate differently from him.

The Active Way:

The magician starts by calling his guide to appear through the medium of the mirror, they engage in conversation and the magician invites his guide to be the filter of his spirit: that is, the magician imagines that his spirit is looking through the spirit of the guide by making use of the magician's own eyes. He acts in the passive way, but is now in a certain position to teach the virtues themselves how to best evolve, to elucidate them, or give them special missions.

Once this is done, the magician follows to the air element, whose ointment is made of hazelnut, juniper berries, rose blossoms and cherry bark.

For the water element: Straw, turnip, sugar beet, peony blossoms and cherry leaves.

For the earth element: Parsley roots, caraway seed, plantago leaves and carnation flower.

When experience has crowned the magician, he will be able to make his magical mirror his central fort of operations, but, unless he falls prey to his own images, he must start from the base, with his behaviour. He must still check his soul mirror via his soul mirror books, now more than ever, lest he falls as the witch of the "Snow-White" tale. Also, the magician's virtues are his angels, governing the many rings of the magician's existence, and whenever he needs to enrich his universe, he may create new virtues and later give them the wings of the Malaki.

Ꙇ tep 18

Unless the magician is unwilling to take the reins of his conscious self, he must always strive to be ahead of his virtues, and even more virtuous than his virtues. That is why Bardon's technique on using the magical mirror for self-influence is important.

Draw so much light that you become like a sun. Focus on a desire and impregnate it with light, for instance intuition, inspiration or any other desired attribute. Have the light flow through your hands onto the glass of the mirror, accumulating there until all of the light has passed into the mirror.

Once this light forms a brilliant white ball of intense rays, the procedure must yet be repeated several times until the rays penetrate our very own body, spirit and soul, releasing the wished influence. By firm conviction, willpower and imagination, we bind this light to the mirror's surface for as long as intended. Once the work is finished, the light is to be dissolved.

This is to become the magician's daily meditation, having him explore the truth ever more deeply and the solutions to any imperfections, then translating it into the representations of the soul mirror and acting upon it.

At night, he is once more to make use of the mirror against any opposition to his progress in the following manner:

> *A magic mirror also can be used as a defensive or protective tool. But then, of course, the impregnation of the emissive power in the mirror is to be modified in a corresponding way...that the rays of the light will detain the undesirable and unfavourable influences or throw them back to the starting point...In all these cases you have to load the impregnation of the mirror or the room with akasha, transferring the quality of intangibility and impenetrability into it imaginatively.*[46]

---

[46] Franz Bardon, *Initiation into Hermetics* (Germany: Rüggeberg-Verlag, 1993), 220.

Now, to fixate his truths and empower the practice of his solutions, the magician will apply the creation of the electromagnetic volt. We have taught the right method to generate the proper radiation of the electric and magnetic fluids, and how to compress them, in the end, at the left and right hands. The magician will, this time, project with his right hand an electric ball of one yard, and, into it, a blue magnetic ball, so that it envelopes the electric red ball layer by layer until it reaches two yards. The centre of the two spheres is the same. When faith and conviction are firm, he impregnates the volt with the concentration of his desire.

Taming of the Pegasus

Once the magician is taking large steps towards perfection, he will place a black card with the fluid condenser behind the glass and consider that the father of all faults is the fear of death, and he is to make it his job to lose that fear. For that reason, he is to use the mirror as suggested by Bardon when the author writes:

> *Sit down comfortably in front of your mirror and load its surface with the akasha,-element which you are sucking into your body by breathing through lungs and pores. The loading of the mirror with the personal akasha can take place whether by your hands or directly via the solar plexus.*[47]

With the method implied in this passage alone, the magician can extend his knowledge of his virtues through the magical mirror by meeting directly with the akashic virtues, and he will witness by such ways powers that he probably never thought he would, but this is not where the work ends.

The magician must still forget his body and think of himself as spirit, able to adopt all shapes and sizes. In this way he is able to enter the mirror and stand on the astral plane. There, the magician must explore without losing consciousness or falling asleep. The magician is to return from the mirror and connect to complete darkness on the astral plane until perceiving light in it, accompanied by an overcoming feeling of spacelessness, freedom and timelessness.

---

[47] Franz Bardon, *Initiation into Hermetics* (Germany: Rüggeberg-Verlag, 1993), 209-210.

Later on the paragraph and most essentially, Franz Bardon finishes:

You will see the place that shall be yours once you have left your physical body. The fear of death will be abolished hereby once and forever.[48]

This is to be the magician's truest place and the indwelling of absolute truth.

[48] Franz Bardon, *Initiation into Hermetics* (Germany: Rüggeberg-Verlag, 1993), 210.

Step 19

At this stage, the magician is approaching god cognition. He is to check off any signs of pride, blind ambition or superciliousness. He is to check on how humble and receptive he still is, including to other persons, for they are tools to keep him grounded. If the magician loses his ground now, all is lost.

Then, the magician will engage in mental wandering, and he will make himself lighter and lighter until he is pushed off the earth, and finally, from where he is, the earth is seen no more. There are to be no stars until there is one. At this point the magician is to concentrate all his willpower in calling forth his guardian genius, whom he has met before, from out of that star. Hand in hand, they are to ascend to higher spheres.

First, he is to be acquainted with the Moon. Several journeys to the moon should take place, and during this period the magician is to check his soul mirror for the faults of glamour, grandiosity, becoming overly convinced of romantic ideas or ideas of self-importance, primitive and raw emotions, being unearthed and taking credit for miracles. He is to check constantly for confusions between the so-called astral experiences and the spiritual experiences: non-physicality brings no holiness or spirituality. As virtues, he may be guided by the qualities of a broader and deeper grasp of life and being, a larger field of view, connection with the racial unconscious of humankind and experience. As subordinate qualities, he may or may not find manifestations of epiphenomena and paranormal power, telepathy, telekinesis, clairvoyance and synchronicities. Signs of success are that the magician's reason is deeply reunited with his instincts, emotions, dreams and visions and the self acquires a sense of cause and effect and of how to influence the chain of events, and the flourishing of sensitivity and empathy takes place.

Secondly, he is to be acquainted with Mercury. Exploring the multiplicity of things, their relations and significant patterns. The organisation of options, memories, experience, information and the extrapolation from the known to the unknown are hardwired into literal and plastic realities there. Abstractions immediately become languages, numbers, geometrics and radiate by expressing logic and science. Signs of success here might manifest as a greater ability for mental exercises. The soul mirror should be searching for bad signs indicating that the mind is still closed to new theories and revisions of all that the magician has learned before. The magician is endangered if his mind closes to methods of confirmation, refutation and testing, for self-importance is identifying with the theories and not allowing the self to identify with truth, evolution and progression. The intellect of the magician expands the more he puts it to use. If the magician keeps expanding the mind without putting intellect to use, the mind isn't strengthened and it ruptures. The virtues here are virtues such as integration, evolution, transformation, organisation, elegant complexity and the proactive solving of problems. The magician is to constantly prevent confusing knowledge with will. Faults will be seen in neglecting one's duties, obsessions with complexity, the distractions and seductions stopping the mind from measuring and finding its own limits and spheres of competence. In fact, it's easier to confuse the planes at Mercury than at the sphere of the Moon although Mercury makes the Sphere of the Moon perfectly clear. But also, Mercury's reason is fruitless without the intuition of the Moon.

At the Venus sphere, we learn of the origin of metalogics and aesthetics. There is the omnipresence of the secret harmony and coherence of art, of union through devotion, in everything and every curve and shape. Signs of success come as the union with one's principles or the objective plastic absorption of abstractions, the illogical and a-logical manifesting in aesthetically pleasing forms. The magician starts to perceive the sensuality of symbols. There are virtues of talented sex, love and art. Vices may be manifest as distracting relationships, personal politics, traits of dominance or submission, misplacements of compassion, thoughts of dependency, mistaking lovers for the divine, and addiction to states of creation.

While the magician and his guide ascend on the spheres, he and his guardian genius become ever more intimate and linked. The magician will immediately be stopped from entering the sphere of the Sun unless he can believe in an intelligence superior to himself. This sphere is the pinnacle of self-knowledge, and therefore the crown of this book. There are many marvels that we shall not speak of, but it will be clear to the magician that he and his genius guide can function as one mind at the sphere of the Sun and that this state can continue at will once back in the earth sphere. Signs of success are that people tend to gather around the spiritual and silent charisma of the magician as an integrated human. Qualities to be practised are those of helping others self-develop and helping to reveal their sources of inspiration and life missions. Faults that may appear are delusions of godhood, addiction to the admiration of followers or other possible vampiric dynamics. If the magician's memory is not well exercised, the experiences he may enjoy in the sphere of the sun will also become fragmented and inconclusive.

At Mars, the magician should keep an eye on how well strength, endurance, perseverance, stamina, discipline and courage, defence and power, alertness and invisibility are being learned and put into practice. Great virtues come as "empowered harmony", "empowered integrity", "empowered charisma", "empowered ethics", "empowered honesty", etc. Faults may go from "corruption" to "absolute corruption".

Jupiter will have the magician training his good judgement on his mundane life, together with long-range planning and intuition. It is the place of inspired decisions and an intimate connection with the cosmos at large and, down on earth, with the workings of communities. You learn how to influence the collective human consciousness. The magician's excellence as a human being should be a priority. The magician will work with qualities such as "vast and boundless generosity", "creating opportunities", "life improvement towards oneself and others", "perfect discernment of individualities and potentialities", "being actual", "making correct decisions," and so on. Faults may range from "taking advantage of others" to other manipulative traits that make use of gratitude, resentment and dependency and allowing others to put their spiritual well being and morals in the magician's hands.

Finally, Saturn is the sphere of the so-called last judgement, and it will make the magician sure that even his greatest achievements or affections are but illusions, but, unless the magician has become entrapped in self-importance, this fact will put the cosmic language at his disposal together with true Understanding. If the magician has deluded himself through his progress and if he is not truly free and does not accept this last judgement, he will at this time perish or be made into a vampire and into a black magician. The human virtues lent by this sphere range from responsibility towards the illusions and the evolution of all things to tending and levity. Grave faults may come from mistaking existence for reality.

The magician is now surely a true Adept. But he must not rest yet. It is not yet time to rest, for beyond Saturn there is divinity in such levels that the only way for the human body to be able to process it is by going down again, into the four elements of the earthzone.

Taming of the Pegasus

The magician will again use the method of meditating with the aid of the mirror in his pursuit of truth and problem-solving perceptions. He is to solve the problems of Omnipotence, Omniscience, Immortality and Omnipresence, and also of how they operate together as fire, air, water and earth. He is to find the truth in each of these four divine qualities and meditate on such truths as to become them entirely during his meditations and then making them embodied. He is also to ask what it means to act against each of these divine principles, and how can he obey each of them in principle without compromising the others.

The magician will then make use of the magic mirror to search for a gnome or several gnomes, they being beings of the earth element. He is not to mistake his virtues distributed through the different elements with such beings, as they belong to different realms. Bardon[49] describes the sprites as carrying lamps of varying luminous power in order to find their way in the kingdom below the earth.

Once we remain convinced of the shape of the gnomes, we can adopt the same shapes mentally and identify ourselves with the earth element by loading the whole shape with the element without accumulation.

It is in this shape that the magician imagines himself sinking down into the kingdom below the earth until deep darkness surrounds him. The magician imagines his lamp illuminating the darkness and becomes accustomed to the dimness, recognizing the beings in his own shape that wish to contact him. There, he observes and waits until being addressed.

The magician is not to put himself in unnecessary danger in any of the elemental kingdoms; by invoking the virtue of supreme victory he will immediately be respected by any salamander. By invoking his well-known quality of absolute power he will instantly be respected by sylphs. Inner

---

[49] Franz Bardon, *Initiation into Hermetics* (Germany: Rüggeberg-Verlag, 1993), 253.

and outer mention of the divine blood will appease any undine. Evoking supreme dominion will paralyse the gnomes or make them servile.

Here, we will have the magician explore this second life, and write down his soul mirror as a gnome upon returning. Some of his virtues attributed to the earth element will be thoroughly tested in their realm, and some vices of the earth element that were dormant might also manifest here in a different manner. For instance, gnomes are usually very self-centred for they practise silence, they have a natural selfishness to them and an instinct towards hoarding the mineral essence. If a gnome is working with a rock he is planning to eventually take the whole mountain into his consciousness. This self centred nature brings apathy to the magician in his human life. Also, the gnome's calm and slow rhythm may translate on the human being as sloth. The gnomes analyse every material structure with their senses and then they start to guide these structures in a certain direction, their analysing mind might translate to human life as the magician becomes overly cerebral and excessive in his control of behaviour. At the same time, let's say that the magician is to compete with an adult gnome in terms of the virtue of respect, he will likely lose at first. The gnomes work the material plane through their respect to existence, so that existence surrenders to them as lover to lover and they can work with the mined gold of reality. They can spend centuries learning the spiritual properties of a gem, opening it as an infinite world of light and information. If the magician is to compete with a mature gnome on this, he will likely lose. A gnome takes responsibility for a tree to such an extent that when it changes he allows himself to change with the tree, a human being has a stronger sense of survival and might more easily pull back. The magician has trained his asanas for hours maybe, but a gnome king can sit still for millennia. They can heal each other through pure tenderness, infusing their lamps with it, and through their lamps gnome magicians can attract gods into their allure. Their silent minds burn with a fervency for acquiring consciousness that no mind distracted by human things can know. Their fascination for the fabrics of reality will make them know the magician's house by heart, while the magician, living on it, is mostly ignorant of the fabrics of his own house. At all these things the magician might easily lose if he was to compete with the greater gnomes in quantity, but our competition will be one of quality and according to his own scale of time. The magician will then work with ardour on his human soul mirror, keeping his human balance still, and on his gnome soul mirror, which correspond to his behaviours inside the elemental kingdom of the earth. The root virtue at this kingdom will be Omnipresence, and faults may be guided by everything that weakens the sense of Omnipresence. The magician is to go from gnome to gnome, mastering greater and greater virtues. Wise and heroic gnomes, the alchemists, can taste polarity with their fingertips and shape fate as a sculptor shapes wet clay, in their silence all faculties come to celebrate union and their actions are living expressions of harmony. An ancient gnome holds an inner memory of earth's evolution since the formation of the planet, he knows what justice really is and how to make the best judgements and from their devotion, the planet shines like a spiritual star in the endless darkness. The mature gnome never compromises his independence, not once, for he sees through all thoughts, desires and wishes and becomes the source of transformation himself. Gnome magicians have both powers and discretions about their powers that the magician must equal. Gnome kings and queens have a strong connection to the supreme source that the magician, even as a gnome, must overcome. Eventually, this will lead him to the palace of the king of kings, standing in the centre of the Earth, whom other gnomes call The Forger of the Stars, and such monarch is to transmit directly the most intense quality there is to the earth element, that of Omnipresence.

At this time, the magician can start practising in his own realm the accumulation of this quality through the magnetic principle.

The water element is then to follow, the rules of our exercise are similar. On the shape of the water sprites, Bardon writes:

> *In the very same way he may look for a water sprite in his magical mirror, and he will find that there exists a significant likeness to a human being. There is hardly any difference to be noticed in shape nor in size. Usually the water sprites-called generally nixies, mermaids, or nymphs-are very attractive females although there are male water-sprites mermen too. As for visits to the kingdom of water, it is not absolutely necessary to adopt the shape of a woman; it is entirely up to the magician to transmute himself imaginatively into a mermaid.*[50]

---

[50] Franz Bardon, *Initiation into Hermetics* (Germany: Rüggeberg-Verlag, 1993), 255.

133

On the method to penetrate the water kingdom, our quoted author writes:

> *Providing the magician is mentally prepared, so that he has impregnated his spirit with water, he may transfer himself to a big lake or ocean, wherever he likes to, and submerge down to the bottom of the water. Here, as well, he will not meet water sprites,but by repeating the experiment many times and according to his vivid desire for communication with these beings, he will finally attract them. At first, he will see only female beings moving about in the same free attitude as human beings do. He will hardly meet an unpleasant mermaid; in spite of the fact that all mermaids are very beautiful, he might, indeed, happen to meet the more intelligent ones, the so-called royal leaders, since here likewise a very peculiar class-consciousness does exist.. The magician will notice that they do not dance all the time as they are generally supposed to do, but that they do a certain amount of work, too.*[51]

The magician will set immortality/eternity as his highest aim on the merman/mermaid soul mirror and know that its mystery connects with that of love. Because the beings of the water element are so seductive, the magician may find that his vice of compliance is resurging, but at the same time, if he becomes shy with the water sprites he cannot progress at all. The pleasures that he will meet may make him negligent once more in his human life, and lazy. While the water sprites like to express beauty and are intense, their beauty and intensity comes from the most relaxed state possible to imagine, they close the doors to any kind of self-presumption and squandering simply because it draws the magician away from their own nature and the language of the magician becomes opposite to their expressions. It will be hard for the magician to compete with the dedication to the now and to the other that the most mundane mermaid possesses, let alone with her power to bond. Their unconditional kindness is actually what makes them dangerous, and the love of the most simple nymph knows no boundaries. Human modesty is yet senseless to them, for they don't do modesty, they are modesty, and mermaids know no forgiveness for they never had anything to forgive. For all these reasons, the magician will find himself perfecting his virtues to the point of becoming them. The

---

[51] Franz Bardon, *Initiation into Hermetics* (Germany: Rüggeberg-Verlag, 1993), 255.

priesthood of the water kingdom sings with such grace and peace that everything joins in the chant communicating with perfect clarity, and the magician must be admitted into performing such liturgies himself. Mature water beings have become intelligent through loving with ecstasy and never without it, for ecstasy gives the emotional intelligence fluidity and, when practised constantly, clears the feelings and sharpens the senses. Mermaid crones have made their emotions into an intellect itself, whose essence is that of happiness, of their senses they have made organs of intuition and mediumistic faculties. The magician fought to become indifferent to others' opinions, but now his achievement will even become a hindrance, for he is to think as if opinions were never meant to influence anything. Mermaid magicians are daring, firm and courageous in their approach to the mermaid queens, whose heart is that of the beating of disclosing mystery, for such magicians risk being dissolved by the queen's magnetism. But the magician is not only expected to learn from them, so that instead of being dissolved he becomes immortal, but he is to breathe in such a way that, at each breath, the whole universe dies and is reborn and all is ever as it ever was.

When the magician reaches the end of his expedition, he has become superior to a Taoist master. Then he is able to accumulate the principle of immortality, after having formulated the magnetic volt.

This will be the time to venture in the elemental kingdom of the air, aiming for the knowledge of Omniscience and an attitude to represent it. About this kingdom, Franz Bardon[52] makes known that the air sprites are beautiful, soft, supple, shy and unsociable, and that they move about as if floating in the air.

At first, the magician may find the temper of the sylphs to be vague, may be frivolous, but this will be the reflection of his frivolity. Their love for information might have the magician gossiping about his human life, and their whirlwind of thoughts may make the magician irascible or impotent. With time, the magician will understand that what appears to him to be a confusion of many simultaneous thoughts is but the sobriety of a highly conscious freedom performed with such dexterity that no thoughts cancel each other or enter into a collision course. This in itself is hard enough to describe, but it must be practised even. Each air prince has the wisdom of all libraries put together and the intelligence of all professional

[52] Franz Bardon, *Initiation into Hermetics* (Germany: Rüggeberg-Verlag, 1993), 256.

mathematicians and computer programmers. The virtues and moralities of our religions are but ridiculous caricatures of their natural ways. In a day they can figure out as much as science has since its beginnings and all their cells are made of pure talent. Their magicians master all laws needing only to give expression to their innate capacities, their assiduity is so sharp that time itself is able to learn from them and their diligence towards being puts the hermit to the most absolute shame. By competing with such spirits under his aerial form, the magician may be admitted to meet with the queens and kings, whose wisdom rules supreme over the atmosphere. Maybe the magician will be allowed the perception of all the wind flows over the atmosphere moving together pushed by the heat of the sun, moulding the earth and flowing the waters, with all that it means and the intelligence behind it. Maybe such ecstasies can lead him to know the cosmic quality of omniscience.

Under the electric principle, the magician will become accustomed to charging himself with such divine quality.

Finally, we move to the elemental kingdom of fire, with the intent of working our way to the initiations of Omnipotence. Here, it was written by Bardon[53] that these beings have a likeness to humans, their faces being smaller and their necks extraordinarily long and thin. They are nervous and fidgety.

After taking the shape of the fire sprite and loading it with fire, the magician descends through a crater of a volcano.

Experiencing the willpower of these beings in their own element is likely to cause seeds of insolence. Their quick intensity is likely to cause instability and irregularity. Their quickness might easily relapse into a lack of conscience in the magician, but if the magician remains dull in the face of the salamanders he might even be attacked.

These beings are, therefore, quick to react to anything opposing their divine jobs or distracting them from pursuing their divine wills, but the lowest human being will learn from this discipline nothing, for his ill interpretations will lead him to empower his hatred, vindictiveness, jealousy and anger. It might also be the case that if the magician's consciousness is not sufficiently expanded, he will interpret volition as

---

[53] Franz Bardon, *Initiation into Hermetics* (Germany: Rüggeberg-Verlag, 1993), 257.

adrenaline, easily becoming addicted, but if he freezes, panic and vertigo will strike him. The quick enthusiasm of the common salamander will make the hyperactive human seem extremely slow in thoughts and reactions. But the magician's speed, as a salamander, is to overcome that of his salamander friend. To the simple salamander, every thought and feeling is a firm command, and the magician will feel that he is too soft at first, but he will harden. The maddening effects of lust spells drink from the salamander's passions more than from the nature of the undine sorceress. In the hands of a simple human, such lust becomes self-destructive, but in the hands of the mature magician, it becomes the fabric of discipline and the pillar for the highest tranquillity. The high brows can reveal the divinity of everything just by thinking of it or looking at it, their eyes irradiate as the sun and the highest successes of the human alchemists will appear now like a caricature. Through their creativity, they can penetrate every layer of consciousness to the extent that even the mature magician feels stupid for not having been able to imagine such layers ever existed to begin with. But the magician will exceed the high brows here. The mouths and ears of the high brows are as one: when they are conjuring, their words swallow the world and recreate it in a single act. There are scholars among the salamanders whose knowledge comes from ecstasy, nothing can stand above the erudite salamander, but still he/she has faith impregnating that nothingness. Because they vibrate very quickly they create from the future to the past, their divine inventions are, in truth, not inventions, for they were stolen from the blocks of divine providence and existed already. All these things and others the magician will be able to accomplish. There are salamander magicians so tough that they have absorbed into themselves the impact of the biggest comets ever to have struck the Earth, so persistent that they have survived the ice ages, and so patient that they have eventually fused with the fire of the stars.

By meeting and becoming equal to many of these, and always manifesting the virtue of absolute victory, is the magician to come to the elemental kings of unshakable will. Salamander kings and queens of a will so strong that they have managed to create life out of darkness. They will lead him to their ruler of rulers, around whom the stars spin the fabric of existence. On the heart of the emperor, locked by seven golden keys, the treasure of all treasures, the secret of Omnipotence.

Once having opened it, Omnipotence is then to be accordingly impregnated on the magician's radiations of the electric fluid.

Step 20

The magician will build a figure with the same methods applied to the figurines of the sanctuary of his sublimated instincts. The figure will have aspects of all the four elemental emperors met by the magician, the different parts are to be impregnated with the four divine qualities to such an extent that, when the magician fixes his gaze on any of them, he enters the trance corresponding to the divine quality. At this point, he is to act as suggested by Bardon,

> *...the object of his adoration not as a mere picture, but as a living being, acting, irradiating with such an intensity as if his personal God were standing real and alive in front of him.*[54]

This God, that now appears before the magician's eyes, enters and fills the magician's body and occupies the space of his soul.

Once this has been sufficiently repeated, the magician's imagination will be able to condense the qualities to such an extent that he becomes the divinity, not remaining himself. When this has become automatic, the magician is yet to accumulate the four divine qualities inside himself, compressing omnipotence into his head, the eternity of love in his heart, omniscience in his nervous system and omnipresence in his sensorial organs.

About techniques similar to this one, Bardon[55] writes:

> *So deep must be this unity with God that, during the meditation, there is no God, neither within myself, nor without, subject and object being molten into one another, so that there is nothing but: "I am God", or as the Indian in his Veda puts it, "Tat twam asi-That Thou art."*

---

[54] Franz Bardon, *Initiation into Hermetics* (Germany: Rüggeberg-Verlag, 1993), 262.

[55] Franz Bardon, *Initiation into Hermetics* (Germany: Rüggeberg-Verlag, 1993), 263.

Having become successful, again, the magician is to enter an akashic trance or stand in front of the mirror and think of the different variations of the four divine qualities, he can even read material books in this way, tapping into the original ideas that formulate the concepts thereby written. He is to explore mythology and find in it different variations of the divine qualities under the names of different Gods. To further evolve in his relation with the four divine qualities, he may make use of such entities and compare experiences with them, and he will be made to know different variations of Omnipotence, Omniscience, eternal love and Omnipresence, so that he can direct these divine qualities in different directions with divine precision.

Taming of the Pegasus

To strengthen his dealings between his own godhood and the gods of different mythologies, the magician is to choose a pantheon. Then he is to enter the divine trance and breathe in the timeless and spaceless love of the cosmos, having it filling his/god's whole body and compressing at the base of the spine as an omnipotent ball of radiating light. While the magician's personal god is doing that, he is to masturbate, and the essence of a deity from that pantheon should impregnate the omnipotent ball, originating from inside the eternal love all around. The sexual stimulation of the personal God should work exactly as when the magician is working with breath: the greater the sexual arousal the stronger the accumulation of the wish, until, at the orgasm, it becomes something similar to the electromagnetic radiation, but the personal god is to insulate it and limit it, literally, to the semen. Using this semen as a fluid condenser the magician will create a figurine of the chosen deity, and have it awake and breathe in the doll. The semen alone, charged in such a way, should do the work. When he has finished running through the pantheon, he creates a second sanctuary similar to one of the saints of sublimated instincts.

Bardon talks of sex magic but dismisses the idea and suggests the reader should do the same. In his time, sex was yet the subject of religious prejudice and looked upon as something secret and forbidden. We think it would be ridiculous to let the magician indulge in giving place to a god but not in the arts of sacred sexuality.

Taming of the Horse

As a final step, and once having attained to godhood, the magician can, just as he took the form of a gnome, an undine, a sylph or a salamander, take on the form of one greater than him in the spiritual hierarchy, the Malach, the original shape of the sun-being. He is to look at himself in a regular mirror, and imagine with all his conviction that what he sees reflected in the mirror, instead of his normal physical body, is a blinding penetrating light like that of the Sun. When this is perfectly clear, the magician transfers it to his own body and turns away from the mirror, keeping absolute certainty in his mind as well as in his sensorial perception that he is the light of the sun, and that his regular body is no more or has become invisible.

Then he is to meditate on introspection, reaching out to his emotions and imagining them to be but an unspeakable concentration of willpower. When it is so, he reaches out to his intellect where he will find only original ideas, the ideas that created and still create the world, there being only causes and no effects. When this becomes reality, he reaches up to his spirit to find the light of all lights, the supreme manifestation of absolute victory. Let him now have absolute victory look down through the sun-body by the medium of this unspeakable willpower and witness the world of original ideas, this may come as the world he was able to witness before from his physical body, except as seen through a divine matrix, or it may appear as the abode of the sun directly. Whatever the case may be, he is able to change any cause and influence or cause any chain of events. He will be able to look down on himself as a human and perceive, all at once, all his lifetimes, past and future. By free will, he is able to isolate certain aspects of this timeline and change their causes, freeing his human self from unwanted karma. This is not all, the possibilities are limitless. But even as a Malak, he has strengths and weaknesses to perfect. With the Malak we leave the magician to his own path, but not before giving him one last key to aid forward movement into something greater.

Taming of the Seven-Headed Horse

Once, the magician learned to meditate on his spirit, composed of fire as willpower, air as cognition, water as feeling, and earth as consciousness, he has learned to think with all four heads simultaneously, then adding a fifth, that of the astral senses and finally, the physical senses. He has brought the six heads to think in harmony. The seventh head is that of the God-Head. The magician has learned this seventh head too, all six heads have bowed to the seventh, and during such trances, the pyramid has become wholly the centre at the top. We will now learn how to articulate the seventh head in a different shape. Let the magician transfer himself to his spirit, his mental body, standing beside his physical body. Let the mental body meditate on the godhood that it has known, calling it forth from out of its depth point. Then, the magician will imagine the God-Head leaving the mental body as the hand leaves the glove. The explorations the magician will be capable of are not possible to describe, but let him gaze on the mental body now, for it will become omniscience itself, and let him look at the astral body and it will become the eternal sea of love, let him look at the physical body, and it will become omnipresence. This is the philosophical stone, said to make its owner capable of feeling the sweeping of all stars, and it is the grail of the scarlet lady kept and carried by the seven-headed beast.

Conclusion

The card of The Sun has been laid to the magician. He has opened the path of splendour between intellect and the material body and he has awakened the tremendous serpent spirit of the astral light. By means of reaching up to the God-Head, he has become as God the Son. By many methods has the magician been introduced to the Inner Sun, the warmth of Original Personality. Just as the human being cannot sustain to look directly at the Sun for long, so needed the magician to reach equilibrium by burning away that fat which is unworthy of the Higher Personality, so as to, in the end, be able to look directly from the Sun instead of directly to the Sun. In the process, he has received the imprint and acceptance of the spirit guides. He became a successful candidate to Beauty and has come to understand the limitations of the intellect and to play them in favour of infinity. The subconscious has become fertile with consciousness. And the unconscious surrendered bare-body to the copious collective consciousness of the cosmic rays.

ppendix

We have learned of the form of the Malak and how to obtain it. If the magician wishes to learn how best to fix it he has but to undergo the twelve following labours, trials such as that of Hercules himself.

I

On the Material Plane

The Malak can shift between the worlds, he is either walking in this matrix or at the sun sphere. Let us make sure that the white horse of bodily illumination allows the Malak as much control as it has given the original form of the magician. The first step is keeping the Malak form at every hour and every minute, watching our thoughts and words for a whole day and preventing the necessary distractions of our mundane day to day from disconnecting us from the state of consciousness of the Malak. It may appear to the magician that he is still firm in his assumption of the Malak, but he will be proven wrong when detecting any selfishness, unkindness, love of gossip and criticism. At last, when the Malak state of consciousness and form goes from thought to action, from action to habit, from habit to character and from character to destiny, the first trial is accomplished.

On the Sun Sphere

In this plane, he is to try hard to recognise form with as much clarity as in the physical plane. The sphere of the sun is one of the hardest in this matter, due to the high saturation of light. He will also see that at the sphere of the sun form is also a dominant and enthroned queen, a being named Cassiopeia, the mother of Christ as the Logos.

The magician is to keep his mind vacant at all times as a Malak while in the sun sphere. If he searches for Cetus in this zone, the undine queen of the sun, he will easily understand how thoughts are the tentacles of the devourer of souls. Souls seem to feed on thoughts but are ultimately devoured by them in sacrifice. At the sun sphere, this can be quite immediate.

The magician's impulse for thought should be focused solely on subduing form and breaking any barriers, lest the light be veiled. This means that form is there, but also not. At last, the magician is to find the invisible, the wise, swift and victorious Perseus as a guide.

II

On the Material Plane

At this point the magician, while a Malak, starts to understand that form is non-form, that self is not-self, that male is not-female and female is not-male. He is not to make any difference between the quality of any form and another, or between any state of consciousness and another, it all being God as the energising life. Soon enough, he will understand, by such ways, how sex is in every manifestation, there being an omnipresent orgy between everything with the whole: that is the thought of God, in opposition to the thought of Cetus. But, if the magician, under the Malak form, wishes to isolate and act directly on a subject, whether it is an object, an animal or a person, he must find the spot where it has rebelled against the whole or sinned against union.

The magician will come to understand that, when speaking out loud, instead of forming words, his thoughts as a Malak will be constituted of light, illumination and sound. Light comes as the impulse of an idea, illumination as the vitalisation of that impulse, and sound as the carnal body of the impulse. The body speaks the words, but the words do not invade the mind. The sound of the voice when words are spoken, in turn, should feel like lightning, hiding a whirlwind of astral activity.

But the challenge remains of testing the state of consciousness of the magician as the Malak against the magician's animal nature. When the entire mind is unintentionally occupied with thoughts of craving for the opposite sex or other animal cravings, and any time there is an incapacity to resist a polar opposite, the Malak is not truly being the Malak and the magician is deceived.

The magician will find out eventually that his body distracts him from the state of consciousness of the Malak when the body considers itself as an isolated island to be redundantly gratified by itself. The instincts of the body can be applied to the service of the group mind, body and soul, or simply to the community. Such instincts will not disrupt the connection between the magician as a man and the magician as a Malak.

We keep stressing that it should be clear in the perception of the Malak-magician that neither spirit nor matter are identified with form and that no form stands in the way of the marriage of both. This is the mystery of the soul, who rides the chariot of form.

On the Sun Sphere

At this time the magician, as a Malak, starts to perceive clearly the three lower kingdoms of the Sun. The minerals in the sun are formations of pure Will, the vegetable life is made of formations of pure Love and the animal kingdom is made of formations of pure Intelligence. As the lord of all three kingdoms, the magician may meet Orion, who breaks plurality and unity to bring forth the light. His wife on the solar sphere is called Eridanus, she looks like a stream of starry eyes and her river song leads the souls to incarnate. Because of it, she is considered the judge of the sun sphere.

III

On the Material Plane

The magician will come to notice that, while before, the images of his imagination were fleeting and shifting with the bewilderment of shape in matter, now they come very clear and fixated. This is due to the vacancy of mind having removed the astral matrix from the pull of matter to be given back to spirit.

His senses will be very clean, perceiving the glory of life even in death, his love will be full of wisdom and his willpower will have merged with the treading of the way, with the Tao. Perseus will start to take an active interest even on the material plane, but the Malak will still be sovereign.

On the Sun Sphere

The light of the magician as a Malak on the sun sphere is to become so dense that he literally becomes a fixed star, his senses reaching out through penetrating radiation. He can always project himself under the previous form. As a star, he will see a silver umbilical cord connecting to the Malak form on the Earth and a red umbilical cord connecting to the physical man, who will appear from this high place as a beast of desire.

IV

On the Material Plane

The magician, as a Malak, is to practise physical realities where instinct is required, so that the Malak reconnects with the necessary instincts on the material plane, well aware of all the cells in the magician's human body. Different physical disciplines may come into play, but most journeys and nights slept in the wild. To his avail, the Malak-magician can evoke Diana and be given tasks. As the instinct of the Malak starts to attune with the earthly instincts, he begins to tap into the divine beehive of the earthzone, the collective instinct of humanity as a whole – and the general collective life - and to make it conscious so that he stands as the individual Malak but with the whole of humanity instantly available to his mind. This will come to pass only if the magician is well established as a Malak.

On the Sun Sphere

On the sun sphere, it is time for the star to start understanding all that is going on in his sphere of radiation through spiritual intuition. As ants that take nest inside a tree, beings of the solar mineral, vegetable and animal kingdoms will seek and enter the star and do mass pilgrimages only to come back again. But a ram with the tail of a fish shall sit on the star's lap and become his subordinate.

V

On the Material Plane

At all times the Malak is to focus on the pituitary gland of the man, and there fix his consciousness. In there, he is to control the body and soul of the man. The pituitary body is twofold, but he blocks the post pituitary lobe where personality exists, and strengthens the ante pituitary lobe, the place of original ideas. This is an especially heroic quest, as the Malak is actually suppressing the magician as an adept and all that he has conquered through strengthening his character and vivifying his willpower and his imagination. This is the time to tame the divine lion, the king of beasts: the adept.

On the Sun Sphere

Here, the task isn't easy either. The star will search at its core for a long ligament of orange and blue etheric string, the blue being the singular will of the star and the orange being its power of generation and regeneration. This ligament has the likeness of the DNA but is wrapped around like a sphere or a brain. It contains all lifetimes of the star, past, present, future and parallel lives, including all the incarnations of the magician. He taps into the memories and breathes the fluid or river of memories into the sphere of light until it can take no more and the fluid, containing all memories, becomes a single experience transmuting the substance of the star. To the ultimate experience, life itself is an illusion, and such a stage should complete this step.

VI

On the Material Plane

This is the time to put, without interruption, the virtues of tolerance, compassion and love into full play. The magician, under the form of the malak, should be able by now to be, literally, in the shoes of everyone around him. He needs not to transplant his consciousness, for the I of the Malak has no boundary of self to begin with. Consciousness transference should occur as naturally as the heartbeats, originating from the virtues above. There will be no loss to him, whom matter herself has acknowledged as a divine son.

On the Sun Sphere

Here, it is time to meet with a solar being named Coma Berenice, the pregnant mother of form who rides a divine centaur.

VII

On the Material Plane

At this point the magician, still choosing to maintain his form as a Malak on the material plane, is to use his eyes solely for the purpose of location. He is not to see actual things with them. Due to his enlightened nature, an atonement will be made with the most mundane things of the world. Sexual attraction will be seen as a means to create beauty, money as a means to share and love. Before, we have installed permanent tolerance, compassion and love, and the consciousness of the Malak has been naturally pouring into the consciousness of everything surrounding him. Now, the Malak acts on it, his presence becomes a blessing: where bias is detected in someone else it is turned to justice, where prejudice is, it turns to good judgement, dullness turns to enthusiasm, stupidity to wisdom, intrigue to straightforward conduct and misguided distrust turns to laughter.

On the Sun Sphere

The Malak has learned a great deal about forms in the sun sphere, and how they are also not-form. Now, the star is to drive itself into the forms, disappearing into them and learning how to ride their diversity as a legion.

VIII

On the Material Plane

This is the time for the Malak to put his knee on the mud and recognize that his roots are on the mortal man. Again, we evoke the soul mirror, but to work with it first the Malak has to look at the magician and recognise any remaining faults. At hands, is the combat with the hydra, the queen of astral larvae. And just as the hydra has nine heads, divided in three sets of three, so will our soul mirror be arranged in such ways.

BLACK MIRROR

Body
Vices of a Sexual Nature: Prudishness, prurience, repression, inhibition, promiscuity.
Vices of Comfort: Possessiveness, bluntness, apathy, narcissism.
Vices of Money: Hoarding, power-thirst, slavery to money, craving, selfishness.

Soul

Vices of Fear: Torment, perplexity, fright, cowardice, fear of ridicule, fear of failure, fear of the unknown, fear of old age, fear of opportunity, fear of death.
Vices of Hatred: Negation, destructiveness.
Vices of Power: Corruption, the desire to dominate others, making power a determining factor of social relationships, harshness, and being self-centred.

Mind

Vices of Pride: Imprisonment, self-exalting thoughts, condescension, personality inclinations.
Vices of Separateness: Prizing the part above the whole, emphasis on diversity over unity.
Vices of Cruelty: Satisfaction in hurting others, evil tendencies, corrosion of the mind, delight in causing suffering, taunting, disparaging, ridiculing.

WHITE MIRROR

Body

Humility: Seeing objectively and recognising shortcomings.

Soul

Courage: To attack the larvae coiled at the roots of one's own nature.

Mind

Discrimination: Discovering the right techniques to fight the hydra.

On the Sun Sphere

The Malak, to whom the matrix of all things is available, calls upon the great serpent of illusion whose giant form runs from the moonzone to the sphere of Mercury and the sphere of Venus. He asks to be tested by the serpent, known to trick Adam.

IX

On the Material Plane

Once, the Malak was a blessing, balancing all around him, transmuting bias into justice, prejudice into good judgement and so on. It is time for him to stop interfering with the business of others. There is truth even to the drug addict, the anorexic, the suicidal. His job is to find that truth, which won't be hard for him to sense and spot, and to focus on that truth alone, strengthening it, for when one cuts one head of the hydra, another grows, and one must attack the hydra as a whole, lifting her from the floor. It is said that truth sets you free. The Malak will apply the same principle to the man that is his root.

On the Sun Sphere

At the central altar of the sun sphere, the Malak will find, if approaching silently, a dragon whose breath is the harmonious music of life.

X

On the Material Plane

It is now time for the Malak to enjoy his own nature, for there is not much left to deceive him. The magician will feel a sense of recovering the wonderment that he felt during his first times under the skin of the Malak, and he will finally be able to allow himself to be the Malak without having to fight for it all of the time.

On the Sun Sphere

Perseus will have not much else to teach the Malak on the Sun Sphere, and will give place to a being that is named after the dolphin. This being is no longer held by physical law and can play with nature. We mean to say that he can materialise or dematerialise things, materialise himself on things, teletransport himself, swim through time and jump from out of the waters to find new spaces. But his rule is that of playing, if he stops playing he stops swimming. The dolphin's subordinate is known by men as the solar eagle that carries an arrow.

XI

On the Material Plane

Effortless identification with every form in every kingdom of nature is the word of order. Let's remember that the Malak doesn't exactly see the world as the magician once did: coming before the software or operational system, the Malak sees the code. This means, altogether, a deeper identification all the while. The magician will know he is failing when he still cultivates feelings or thoughts of distrust, and when people or animals turn unexpectedly against him, for it is a sign that he has shown them reasons to feel separate.

On the Sun Sphere

The star removes any remaining sense of importance to its individuality and drops the consciousness of the self so that personality becomes no more than a mechanism. Again, let us remind the magician that personality here takes place on a different scale, for the personality of a star is not the same as the personality of a human animal. Once this is done, the former star becomes That, a consciousness of all that is, so that the Malak is now the sun sphere or, for the first time, truly on the sun sphere.

XII

Again the difference between the solar sphere and the material plane blurs. The adept is the sun, in whatever plane it may be. And he speaks through the silent meditations of all living creatures to the group mind. Not ever, not once, is the magician to expect any recognition on Earth, it is not likely that he will get it, even if he is remembered through the ages for still great but lesser things. In any case, the sun does not expect, and its surface holds no shadows. The feet of the magician walk with the Tao, the heart has saved himself and serves in silence, and his flesh is mortal but already immortal by the virtue of its aspirations. He speaks through the same mouth as all beings and through the same mouth is he recognised by the intelligences of Andromeda, who are matter and who have conquered matter, becoming truth.

Final Observation

In one of my conversations with one of my colleagues, the magician and doctor Shreeram, I realised that I haven't, for reasons of discretion, put in this work any direct observation on the ultimate nature of duality as I consider it to be. As I see more and more students of Franz Bardon fall into its trap, I would like to rectify that. In universal terms, there is no good or bad, there is polarity, positive and negative. Good and bad is a fabrication of knowledge, while the divine admits only to divinity. Sometimes, when Franz Bardon speaks of positive and negative traits in the soul mirror, he is not referring to universal aspects such as would be the case of active and passive traits, he is indicating good and bad traits instead. What makes something divine turn good or bad is subject to decision, action and perception. Meditation on this cross and on this crucible is essential to truly understand the use of the soul mirror.